ENDORSEMENTS

"There's a reason why Scripture uses adoption as metaphor for our relationship with God. JT's personal story brings that connection to life. *The Orphan, the Widow & Me* probably won't take you long to read, but its impact just might last a lifetime."

> —Dave Ramsey, best-selling author and nationally syndicated radio show host

"A poignant story of life – strain, celebration and sorrow intertwined, ultimately revealing that all we experience can be not only redeemed, but also redemptive. JT Olson's story shows that our greatest hurt can become the source of God's greatest gifts through us to others."

> —Jedd Medefind, President of the Christian Alliance for Orphans and author of *Becoming Home*

"JT Olson is a shining example of the journey from success to significance. The first half of JT's life prepared him well for Both Hands. Every family and church passionate about living out James 1:27 should know about Both Hands. Let JT be an inspiration to every man and woman yearning for more than success."

> —Bob Buford, best-selling author and founder of Leadership Network and The Halftime Institute

"As a friend of JT's for over 20 years, I've seen firsthand the power of *The Orphan, the Widow & Me*. His story of loss and gain and submission to the Holy Spirit to do what he is uniquely gifted to do for orphans and widows is one only God could script. READ THIS BOOK and you will be inspired to make a difference too!"

> —Marty Roe, lead singer of Diamond Rio

"Lifesong has seen the incredible impact Both Hands has made for orphans, widows and adoptive families across the country. JT's story is inspiring and we encourage all of our adoptive families to consider a Both Hands project!"

> — Gary Ringger, Lifesong for Orphans

"What a gift to read the life story of a man and ministry that we love and admire! This is a great read for anyone that is searching for a way to see how their life experience can spur on a serious faith journey and get you out of your comfort zone. In his book, JT has a way of calling you to ACTION with the whispers that you have heard from Christ but have ignored. This is a 'curl up and not put down story' that inspires."

> —Suzanne Mayernick and Gwen Oatsvall, Founders of 147 Million Orphans

"*The Orphan, the Widow & Me* serves as a powerful reminder of the impact one person can make when they have enough faith to face their fears, listen to God's call and use their talents and experiences to change the world."

—Julie Gumm, author of *You Can Adopt Without Debt*

"JT Olson is living an adventure, however, adventurous living doesn't come without risk. Trading the certainty of the gold watch, and a comfortable retirement, JT said 'Yes!' allowing God to use his unique skills and life experiences to change the world. If you're looking for an adventure, then read on. If you're risk averse and afraid to really go for it then this book is not for you."

—Greg Murtha, Founder of Leading with a Limp

"I don't know why some people are struck with losses that are tragic and inconsolable. And I don't know why some find that in time the gains, the joy, and the delight born of those dark days are immeasurable. I only know what I know. And I know JT Olson is one of those people. You'll need both hands to read this story, one for the book, the other for a tissue. His story puts flesh and blood on Solomon's words… 'The generous man will be prosperous, and he who waters will be watered himself.'"

—Lloyd Shadrach, Teaching Pastor of Fellowship Bible Church

"There is a saying, 'more is caught than taught.' People hear more of _what we do_ than _what we say_. JT & Sara work hard to let their lives mirror what they believe. I've watched both since their days in college and they seek God's will for their lives daily. You can trust the words shared in this book are from JT's heart more than his head. He is that kind of man. Read with confidence and trust that you are hearing how he is living."

—Allen Clements, former Senior VP, Southwestern Company

"Here is a tale that both captivates and inspires. I dare you to not be moved to action after reading this."

—Jeff Goins, best-selling author of *The Art of Work*

The Orphan, the Widow & Me

Paying It Forward with **Both Hands**

JT OLSON

Manufactured in the United States of America

Published by Both Hands Press

Hardcover ISBN: 978-0-9982830-0-5
Paperback ISBN: 978-0-9982830-1-2
eBook ISBN: 978-0-9982830-2-9

TABLE OF CONTENTS

To my Mom & Dad
(Othello & Lora Mae Olson)

My Aunt & Uncle
(Marie Ann & Ralph Seifert)

And to Sara, my wife, best friend and lover.
The unsung hero of Both Hands.

FOREWORD

Steven and I have known JT and Sara for many years now. Only God knew the many ways our hearts would be woven together by the work that we all love: caring for the least and vulnerable.

Several years ago at a Bethany Christian Services fundraiser, we were able to first spend time with Sara and JT and heard their story of how God had brought them to the place of feeling called to adopt a child. It was obvious at that point that we were kindred spirits with our passion for adoption. We began praying for them, that God would make adoption possible and that they would be able to give a permanent home and family to a child that otherwise wouldn't have one. We also heard from them and saw in their eyes an enthusiasm to help other people adopt as well. I believe that God allowed Steven and me to SEE these early seeds that were planted—something that would eventually grow into Both Hands.

As time has gone on, JT and Sara have been amazing advocates and supporters of adoption. After their own adoption was final, we watched as their passion continued to grow to help other people adopt. From giving of their own time and money to support adoption organizations, to counseling women who were thinking about terminating unplanned pregnancies, JT and Sara have literally been the hands and feet of Jesus in the Kingdom work of adoption and orphan care. Steven and I have considered it a privilege to cheer them on in this most important work of caring for orphans and widows.

Most people would assume that with loss comes the possibility for bitterness to take root. Experiencing loss and wrestling with faith, JT's heart wrenching story is one of a young man determined to battle the enemy and push back the darkness. The enemy was truly defeated! God's hand is evident in JT's entire story from his childhood, his career path, and through raising his own children. The recounting of his and Sara's adoption journey gives a firsthand perspective on the many joys and trials that often accompany the adoption process. I so appreciate JT's ability to paint a realistic picture of what adoption and its challenges can look like. This book is a great resource for anyone thinking and praying about adoption becoming part of their own story.

God is so clearly evident in JT's life and was working through many life events ultimately leading to the founding of Both Hands, an organization that cares for both widows and orphans. Allowing God to direct his people, and then having the faith to take those steps, this story tells of what God longs to do through people who love Him. I love JT's tenacity and strength. I encourage you to go on this journey with him as he tells this amazing tale of hope and faith. JT show's all of us how to steward the story that God gives us, and in doing so it proves that out of the ashes, beauty will rise, and Kingdom work can be accomplished.

> Until All are Home,
> Mary Beth and Steven Curtis Chapman

The Chapmans are the co-founders of Show Hope, one of the largest adoption grant organizations in the country. Mary Beth is also a New York Times best-selling author and Steven is a Grammy Award Winning Recording Artist.

Whenever I've told the *Both Hands* story, somebody comes up to me afterwards and says, "You should write a book." …So we did.

CHAPTER 1

Are Mom and Dad Home?

When people ask me where I'm from, I start with Iowa and hope for the best.

"Anywhere near Des Moines?"

"Um, not exactly. Are you familiar with Decorah, Luther College?" That usually gets some sort of recognition, but most people have never heard of Harper's Ferry, Iowa.

Any history buff has heard of Harpers Ferry, but that's the one in West Virginia. That's the one where abolitionist John Brown led a raid on a federal armory, which became a catalyst for the Civil War.

No, the Harper's Ferry where I grew up hugs the west bank of the Mississippi River, just across from Wisconsin. Among the many things that distinguish us from the other Harpers Ferry is the fact that we had the good sense to use an apostrophe in our name. In fact, that may be our only claim to fame because both then and now, you would not describe Harper's Ferry as bustling.

However, it is beautiful, with the bluffs along the river and in the fall, it'll take your breath away.

In the 1950s, approximately 250 residents lived in Harper's Ferry. Over the past fifty years or so, the village has added another eighty residents. In the summer, I think the population shoots up to about 1500 because it is a great place to spend a vacation. The closest big city—twenty-five minutes west—is Waukon, population, about 4,000 give or take a few. It serves as the county seat of Allamakee County, and home to the Allamakee County Fair, where many of my friends showed their animals and got to hang out in the show barns for the week, spending their year's savings on foot-long hot dogs, hand-squeezed lemonade, and car-amel-covered apples. Since ours was a working farm, we didn't have much time for the fair, save for the annual visit to walk the midway, take our chances on the ring toss and shooting gallery, and of course, go for a spin on the Tilt-a-Whirl or the Scrambler.

Because of the distance, you made your trips to Waukon count—no driving into town to pick up a pound of coffee. So about once a week we would go to Quandahl's Food Ranch and stock up on whatever we did not grow or raise. I especially loved it when Dad or Uncle Clifford headed up these excursions because after all our necessary shopping was done, they would stop at the S and D Café or maybe Wally's Cafe and order a slice of pie for all of us. What a treat!

My Dad, Othello, was a proud Norwegian farmer. His forefa-thers had come to Iowa around 1850 and bought the farmland sometime around 1853. He and Uncle Clifford were partners in farming. They were two of the five children born to John and Sophie Olson. Dad was born in 1910 and along with the other Olson kids, went to school in a one-room schoolhouse about a mile from our house, right where the gravel road hits the blacktop.

He met my Mom when he was forty-one years old and she was twenty. Lora Mae Daley was a student at Luther College when one of the girls on her dorm floor took her home for the weekend. It was at a little country church during that weekend when she ran into my father, the Norwegian bachelor farmer.

Now Mom was from a somewhat well-to-do family in Wauwatosa, a suburb of Milwaukee, so you can imagine the scandal when this young girl started to date a farmer twice her age, and a year older than her own father. I've read the stack of letters that they sent to each other during their courtship and it's a beautiful love story. An older man, just not believing that someone so young and beautiful could be interested in him and a young college coed smitten with this handsome (I'm told I resemble my dad) middle-aged farmer. The story has all the ups and downs you would expect from a romance with these dynamics, including a not so happy father, 200 miles away in Milwaukee. Decorah was only forty miles away, so I'm betting that my mom and dad saw each other a little more often than my grandfather would have liked. As I said earlier...scandalous!

Eventually they got married on March 21, 1953, and my mom became a farmer's wife. Mom was a driver. She got things done. I think she brought some order to the farmhouse where these two bachelors lived, and maybe raised the bar a little bit at mealtime too.

Apparently, she adjusted to farm life pretty well and over the next ten years, she and Dad had five kids, three boys and two girls.

We farmed 380 acres of some of the most beautiful land in all of Iowa. People think of Iowa as flat, joking that you can stand on a picnic table in Davenport and see Des Moines, 175 miles to the west. Not so where I grew up. Our little corner of northeastern Iowa reminds me of the rolling hills of Tennessee's Cumberland Plateau. In fact, the terrain between Waukon and the Mississippi River is the steepest along the entire Iowa bank of the Mississippi.

In those days, you could almost survive on the kind of farming we did, which was a combination of crops and livestock. The corn, oats, and hay provided the food for our herd of Angus beef cattle and Hampshire hogs, and everyone pitched in a hand to make sure the crops got planted and harvested, and the animals got fed. Most mornings, before school I and my brothers would head out to the barn to help feed the livestock, then race back inside our modest farmhouse for breakfast. The bus stop was at the end of a long, winding lane, so by the time we climbed aboard that big yellow limousine, we were pretty bushed. But that was okay, because the forty-five minute ride to school gave us plenty of time to recover. Or more likely, to catch up on the homework we put off the night before.

Yet even with everyone helping out so Dad wouldn't have to hire extra help, farming alone didn't provide enough income to support our family. So on the side, my dad sold Lutheran Brotherhood life insurance as well as specially treated oil that farmers used on their cows to keep their coats looking good. In the rest of his "spare time," he worked as a carpenter. Every once in a while, he and a couple of his friends—Olaf and Melvin—got hired to build a new shed or add a room to someone's house. In addition to my parents and siblings, Uncle Clifford, my dad's brother, lived with us. Eight people living in a 1,500 square foot home. By today's standards, that home was way too small for eight people, but we didn't know it at the time. Eventually, Mom decided we needed some extra room, so Dad and his buddies built an extra room off our living room. Working the farm and taking on all that extra work may seem excessive, but that's how family farms survived. You were willing to do whatever it took to put food on the table.

If I told you we had Olivers, you will be forgiven for scratching your head, but the tractors on our farm were made by the Oliver Farm Equipment Company, and thus called "Olivers." Or what farmers refer to as "the other green," as opposed to the more popular (today) John Deere tractors which are also green. I didn't know it at the time, but Olivers were the first tractor powered by a diesel engine and for years outsold John Deere. But it really didn't matter that much to me, because when you're a kid on a working farm, the big attraction was being able to drive before you had a driver's license. I started driving our Olivers when I was nine years old, and I would have been just as happy if they were Allis-Chalmers or Massey Ferguson. A tractor was big and powerful and made the coolest roar pulling a wagon with a 100-bale load of hay up one of our sloping fields. Farm kids didn't have much on city kids, but we could drive and they couldn't.

I can't think of a better way for a kid to grow up than on a working farm, but it wasn't all fun and games. Baling hay may sound romantic, but imagine throwing thirty to forty pound bales high up into a barn where the temperature soars over a hundred degrees, and you have to wear a long-sleeved shirt to protect you from the scratchy hay. There's an art to it. You have to put both hands on that bale, get your feet positioned right and then heave-ho. A lot like those fancy workouts everyone does nowadays, but we just called it farming. And then there were mornings when the temperature hovered around zero and you had to drive the tractor through one or two feet of snow to haul hay out to the cattle. In the dark. Before school. I mean, I've got some real stuff to brag to my kids about how tough it was growing up… half mile walk to the bus, uphill, in the wintertime…that kind of stuff.

I can't think of a better way for a kid to grow up than on a working farm, but it wasn't all fun and games.

But overall, the good easily outweighed the bad. When I wasn't helping out or going to school, I had plenty of fun. Our farmhouse was surrounded by pasture and crop fields to the west, and woods to the east. One of my favorite things to do was to head down this little valley the other side of the corncrib and then walk to the woods where I could just hang out for hours. I especially loved it in the spring when the snow and ice was melting. I'd build dams in a little stream or crunch through the ice. Later in the summer I would head further back into the woods where the stream opened up into a pool that ran into a cave, and I'd jump in and swim into the cave. But mostly I just loved hiking through the woods. We had a couple of ponds, but I steered clear of them because Dad told us there was a mad cow near them. I think that was just his way of keeping us away from the ponds, and it worked.

Television wasn't much of a distraction for two reasons. One, we only got two channels on our black and white TV. If we wanted to watch NBC, we turned our antenna to the west. For CBS, we turned it to the north. But the biggest reason I didn't watch much television is that my mom did her best to limit our time in front of it. Still, I found time to watch my favorite program, *Dr. Max*, out of Cedar Rapids. He had all kinds of cartoons and of course, the finest in entertainment, *The Three Stooges*. Now that's culture! Although Mom never saw the light on that one.

Don't ask me how we survived without video games, smartphones, and the Internet, but somehow we did.

By today's standards we were probably on the lower end of the middle class, but I never felt deprived. Just the opposite. When you raise pork and beef and have a big garden, you eat pretty well. And often. Breakfast at six a.m., a big snack at ten. Then lunch at noon. And somehow we ate again around four p.m., followed by the big dinner around six. And we were all pretty skinny, despite all the rich food. Farm work can do that to you.

Dad also always kept a cow bred and every morning went out and milked her while the rest of us were doing chores. I would not share this with a cardiologist, but you haven't lived until you've had your bowl of oatmeal or cereal slathered in fresh cream that we skimmed off the top of the milk pail. I don't think I ever heard of two-percent milk until after I was married, and when I first saw a glass, it looked so thin I thought someone had diluted real milk with water.

Sundays were the one day we didn't work that much, except for the daily chores. We were Lutherans, so as soon as we got our chores done, we got cleaned up, packed ourselves into the family sedan, and drove to the Old East Paint Creek Lutheran Church, where my mom and dad first met. I think it was the first Lutheran church built west of the Mississippi. As tiny as it was quaint, this classic white-sided country church was the only church I knew. My dad not only sang in the choir, but at one point, was also the president of the congregation. When I was in sixth grade, my parents graciously spared me the details, but apparently my dad and the pastor butted heads, resulting in us leaving that church, transferring to St. John's Lutheran in Waukon. The longer drive did not dampen my parents' involvement. Dad continued to sing in the choir and Mom was involved in a Bible study for women. And even though very few sixth-grade boys got excited about going to church, I didn't mind. I liked the chance to be with kids my age and learned to appreciate the slower pace that Sunday represented.

Every now and then, my mother would volunteer us three boys to sing at one of the local retirement centers, The Good Samaritan Home. She made us wear matching clothes and I guess we were "The Olson Boys." It seems like we always sang "What a Friend We Have in Jesus." Not sure if that was because it was such a recognizable song, or if that was the one Mom knew best.

So Mom played the piano, and she, of course, wanted to share that joy with her kids. Now at first, I was excited to start piano lessons. I was in second grade and for the last two years had watched my two older brothers John and Jim, (yeah, we're an all 'J' family) take lessons. How I envied them. The first year went okay and I performed the perfunctory "Indian Hunter" piece at the recital. It was all cool, not exactly Liberace, but acceptable. Here's the rub: Mom always had us practice for thirty minutes every day, five days a week. There were some torturous moments at the Olson household with my mom doing her best to enforce what was really a pretty good idea, if you want to get good. But thirty minutes a day cuts into Three Stooges time, which I didn't appreciate. I put up with it for another four years, but for Christmas in 1968, my Dad let me quit. Good deal for him, good deal for me, and yes, to any young people reading this, I regret I quit. Something from that musical endeavor stuck with me though, because to this day, I can still play my last recital piece…"Swing Time on Young MacDonald's Farm."

One day, my parents announced that they were going to be gone for a few days, something that almost never happened. Farming doesn't offer too many opportunities to get away, but their sixteenth wedding anniversary was coming up and they wanted to do something special. They had arranged for my two little sisters, Julie and Jerene (the other J's), to stay with friends, while Uncle Clifford would do his best to ride herd over us boys—John, Jim, and me. They planned to leave on Thursday for Mount Horeb, Wisconsin and check in to the Karakahl Country Inn—not exactly a five-star hotel, but a pretty nice place for a farm couple from Iowa. They would be joined by my Mom's college roommate and her husband, Jo and Jerry Carlstein, who were very close friends of the family and whose anniversary was a day later than Mom and Dad's. On Saturday they would drive back so they could be in church the next day.

The appointed Thursday found me running late for school, and I had no desire to walk the half-mile to our bus stop in the biting March wind. Dad was just coming up to the house from the barn, so I asked him to drive me to the bus stop.

"You've got plenty of time—just get going," he encouraged. "You'll make it."

Not real happy with his answer, I gave him the standard teenage response which probably included, "But Dad, you don't understand. Come on, just take me."

His response was, "Just go on. You can make it, if you run." And then he warmly added, "Goodbye, I'll see you in a few days."

My only response was an angry, "Bye!" And I took off running.

I was so angry that he couldn't take the few minutes to drive me to the bus stop, unable to understand the reality I later embraced as a father, that he probably had things to do before getting underway on his anniversary trip. I made the bus, but I was hot.

By the time I got to school, I had simmered down and looked forward to being home alone with just my brothers and the coming weekend, which, perhaps to give Uncle Clifford some relief, included spending Saturday afternoon with neighbor friends. So after we finished our chores Saturday morning, Uncle Clifford dropped us off at the Goettel's farm where we ran off to the barn for an afternoon of building forts and playing hide-and-seek. And as always, we had a blast, made even sweeter by the fact that my *Are Mom and Dad home?* "girlfriend" joined us. For a twelve-year-old just discovering girls, this was a dream Saturday. But like all good things, it came to an end around five when John Goettel drove us the three miles back to our place.

I was filthy from playing pretty hard in the barn, so I headed straight for the basement to clean up. I plopped down on a chair at the bottom of the stairs and was starting to unlace my boots when I looked up to see John, his eyes red as if he'd been crying. My first thought was that he must have gotten in trouble with Mom for playing with us in the barn. He'd recently had hernia surgery and wasn't supposed to do anything active for a few more weeks. I just thought he'd just been confronted by Mom. I understood the tears. I pretended not to notice—after all, what guy likes to be caught crying—so instead I asked, "Are Mom and Dad home?"

In that innocent question on March 22, 1969, my life changed and would never be the same.

"Mom and Dad are dead."

CHAPTER 2

Suddenly an Orphan

I completely missed the clues.

John Goettel normally was talkative, fun loving. On any other ride with him, he would talk and joke with us. But this short trip from his place to ours was different. Quiet. Almost somber. I didn't realize it at the time, but he knew. Uncle Clifford had called him: "Get the boys home. There's been an accident. Don't say anything to them just yet."

Then there was the truck in the driveway, not the least bit unusual. Everyone drove a pick-up truck, so this could have been another neighbor stopping by to see Uncle Clifford. Except this truck had a red light on top. How could I have not noticed the county sheriff's truck? But I guess you miss stuff like that after a fun day with your friends.

When you add up the ride home in silence, the sheriff's truck, and John's red eyes, I should have known something big was up, which was why it's almost surprising that those words hit me like a freight train, but they did.

"Mom and Dad are dead."

I didn't know what to say, so my first response was, "What?"

"Mom and Dad are dead. They were killed in a car accident an hour ago." Then he turned around and walked upstairs.

I collapsed—I literally fell to the bare cement floor of our basement wailing like an injured baby calf. All the signs made sense. This wasn't some sick joke John was playing on me. The sheriff got the news and drove straight to our place and told Uncle Clifford. He called John Goettel. As I was in the basement taking off my boots, John was getting the news from Uncle Clifford. And now it was my turn to find out.

Although I did not have words to describe it then, I had just become an orphan.

As I cried and cried on that cold floor, all I could see in my mind was a picture of Dad and us kids on the Mississippi River, water skiing. One of my favorite things to do. I saw my dad smiling and having fun with us and now I knew he was gone. For good. I'd never see him or my mom again. Although I did not have words to describe it then, I had just become an orphan. And the loss was suffocating, unreal, like a bad dream you can't shake.

I cried until I ran out of tears and eventually trudged upstairs. The sheriff was still there and Uncle Clifford was on the phone letting other family and friends know, which explains why in his distraction he'd not been by my side to comfort me. He was grief stricken and could barely talk himself. He had lived with us as far back as I could remember, and my brothers and sisters and I were his life.

As a young man, Clifford had been engaged to a girl from town. One day in a twist of fate, his hand got caught in a piece of farm machinery, severing the ends of his fingers and leaving him with roughly half a hand. To our disappointment, she broke off the engagement with him, despite the fact that his injury never stopped him from doing as much work as anyone else. I don't think he ever got over it. We had become his family, and now? Now what?

Listening to bits and pieces of his phone calls and the conversations of others around me, I learned that Mom and Dad had decided to visit a friend in Spring Green, Wisconsin, on their way home from Mt. Horeb. As they left and headed out onto Highway 14, a pick-up truck crossed the center line and crashed head on into Dad's car. A grandfather who had his grandson with him drove the truck. If I remember correctly, the grandson died and the Grandfather went to the hospital and he recovered. My parents were killed instantly. I remember taking some solace in the fact that they went together and they probably didn't suffer, but we did.

As the word spread, our house filled up quickly as neighbors and relatives rushed over to offer support. That's one of those great things about rural life—everyone knows everybody and in situations like this they just want to help out in some way. They come with both hands open and ready to pitch in. Of course, every time someone came into the house, we all started crying again. I don't think I've cried as much in my whole life as I did those next few days. It was just so sad. People would walk through the front door and head for one of us kids and just hug us and weep with us. They didn't say much. Didn't have to. We knew that they felt our loss almost as deeply as we did.

One person did say something, however. Something I found extremely comforting. Our pastor had, over the years, become more than a pastor to my dad. They were great friends. So when Pastor Voeller came by, it got real quiet as he opened his big Bible and began reading the 23rd Psalm: "The Lord is my shepherd, I shall not want..." I was no more or less religious than any of the other Lutheran kids who went to church every Sunday, but hearing those words sort of made sense of my faith; made me appreciate that there was a God who "restoreth my soul." I could relate to the green pastures and still waters, and had taken refuge there many times. After reading those beautiful words of King David, Pastor Voeller then prayed for each of us kids by name. I don't remember what he said in his prayer, only that it felt good to hear our pastor praying for us. I was likely in a state of shock by then. Numbed by the grief that invaded my very being. But Scripture and prayer gave me comfort.

Some of the adults talked with Uncle Clifford, who was clearly distraught. They wisely decided that we kids would be better off that first night if we had some other place to stay. I don't recall where the rest of my siblings went, but I was sent home with the only first cousin on my dad's side of the family, Kurt. We were pretty close to his family, so that made sense. The next day was a Sunday, I woke up thinking maybe this was all a bad dream, but the sickening realization dawned on me. It wasn't a dream. It was real. I wasn't going to see Mom and Dad again this side of heaven. It was surreal—one day I've got a great mom and dad; the next day they're gone and we're all orphans. I didn't realize it, but good parents are like a foundation that keeps you tethered in life. When that just vanishes in one moment, you feel like you're just floating, with no direction or hope. It's just plain sad and painful. The ultimate paradigm shift.

I wasn't going to see Mom and Dad again this side of heaven.

I didn't go to church, but the parents of my best friend, Greg Hamm, dropped him off so that I at least had someone my own age to hang out with. It was a sweet gesture of the Hamms, but also a little awkward. Two twelve-year-old boys sitting in a room after one of them had lost both parents. It likely went something like this:

"I'm really sorry about your mom and dad."

"Um, thanks. Me too."

Silence.

"How'd it happen anyway?"

"Bad crash. That's all I know."

"Oh man. I'm really sorry."

"Thanks. Me too."

More silence. Like I said, a bit awkward, but comforting nonetheless.

Between variations of that same conversation repeated a few times and lots of silence, we got through it. Actually, it felt good to be with someone my own age, and Greg was my best buddy. Even if it was a little awkward, it was sure better than being around all those adults. Not that the adults weren't kind and understanding, but they all felt they had to do something to make me feel better. My Aunt Agnes, my dad's sister, even asked me if I needed a laxative. Just what a twelve-year-old boy wants to talk about with his aunt. Older people just think about different things than kids do. I assured her that everything was working properly and that I would be okay.

While it was good to get away from the house, I was happy when Kurt dropped me back off at our farm later that day. My brothers had gotten back also, and we were joined by my Uncle Ralph and Aunt Marie Ann, my mom's sister. They had driven in from Milwaukee that morning. My mom and Aunt Marie Ann were about as close as two sisters could be and so our families were close too. The friends who were taking care of my two little sisters had actually heard about the accident on the radio and drove down from Decorah, about forty miles away. So when they arrived, my Uncle Ralph and Aunt Marie Ann had to sit down with the girls and try to explain that their mommy and daddy had been killed in a crash. Fortunately, they were too young to realize the gravity of the situation. In fact, when Aunt Marie Ann told them they would be living with them my little sister, Julie, said, "Does that mean we get to ride in your blue station wagon?" A little much needed levity to the situation but it confirmed that they really didn't get it. It just seemed so sad to listen to them tell my little sisters such horrible news. Hearing them explain all that just made me realize that things are definitely going to be different.

Over the next few days, people kept showing up and doing nice things for us. My grandpa on my mom's side pulled up in his big white Cadillac convertible, and it reminded me of the times he would surprise us at school and give us a ride home with the top down. Then Ozzie Quandahl, who owned the local grocery store, arrived with his arms loaded down with bags of groceries. Neighbors kept a steady stream of food coming—I don't think I ever ate better in all my life. And yet, as nice as it was to be surrounded by so many good people, I was pretty much in a daze through it all. A question lingered in the back of my mind, but I couldn't ask it. I think maybe I was afraid of the answer I would get. I instinctively knew things would eventually get back to normal, but what would normal look like, now that Mom and Dad were gone? More specifically, what was going to happen to us kids now?

I'm pretty sure my parents had never discussed their final wishes with Uncle Clifford, so he had to wing it when it came to making preparations for the funeral, though Pastor Voeller likely offered some guidance. Maybe not enough, for when Monday rolled around and we had to go to the funeral home for the visitation, I was surprised to discover it would take place at the Bakke Hansen funeral home instead of Martin Brothers. Bakke Hansen catered mostly to Catholics while Martin Brothers handled the Protestant funerals. And in those days, Catholics and Lutherans didn't always see eye to eye. I didn't realize it at the time but I have since come to enjoy the fact that God seems to have a sense of humor and probably had His hand in that decision.

When it was time to go to the funeral home for the visitation, I remember being just a little scared and apprehensive. I'll never forget, though, walking into that funeral home and seeing my mom and dad lying in their caskets. I don't think I'd ever seen a dead person before, and here I was looking at my own parents. That's probably when it sunk in for me. They really weren't coming back.

We stayed at the funeral home until late Monday night because so many people came to pay their respects and supports us. My dad wasn't the most successful farmer in the county, but he was a good man, well-liked by everyone. A school board member, active in church, and always one of the first to arrive when another farmer needed help. Mom was just as active in the community and church. She was always serving folks and lending a hand. Having so many people come and offer encouraging words to us and demonstrating how much they loved my parents spoke volumes to me about the kind of impact my mom and dad had on the community.

The next day, March 25, 1969, we left the house in a cold drizzle and headed to St. John's Lutheran Church for my parents' funeral, and again, I was struck by how many people turned out on such a miserable day. The place was packed, with people spilling out into the foyer and sitting on the steps. I'm sure it was a beautiful funeral—if funerals can be beautiful—but I don't remember a thing. All I remember was walking behind the caskets at the end of the service and being so sad and wondering, "What's going to happen now? Who will take care of us? Would we all stay together or would we have to go live with different people?" I loved my mom and dad and I only wished that my last conversation with Dad wasn't one that I was so mad at him.

What's going to happen now? Who will take care of us?

By Wednesday, the day after the funeral, things sort of got back to normal. All five of us kids were together at the farm. My Aunt Marie Ann and another aunt—Ginny—stayed for the next two weeks because if the cooking was left to Uncle Clifford, we'd have starved. Of course, we were still reeling from our loss, but Aunt Ginny, not really an aunt, but just a great friend of the family, provided the comic relief that we all needed. She was a hoot and brought joy with her wherever she went, and if there was one thing we needed, it was a lot of joy. I still laugh when I think of the way she would break into one of the songs that was popular on the radio in those days, for no reason other than that she could. The one I always remember was a Neil Diamond hit: "Pack up the babies and grab the old ladies, and everyone goes, cause everyone knows, Brother Love's show." Aunt Ginny was an attractive woman—fifty years old—and she would often laugh, "I'm a hot fifty-year old!" She was that way normally, but I'm pretty sure she knew how much we needed to laugh and gave it a little extra color during those two weeks with us.

Believe it or not, we all went back to school the day after the funeral. And was that ever weird. I tried to act like nothing had happened because when you're in the seventh grade, you don't want to be different. Yet I was so conscious of the fact that everybody was looking at me. No one talked about it. No one. I don't recall a single teacher pulling me aside and saying something or even acknowledging that I had just lost both parents. It was just so strange. It would have been awkward if they had. It was awkward that they didn't.

But there was one person who spoke to me about my loss, and that was my Sunday school teacher, Mrs. Adams. Her husband was the associate pastor of our church, and they were obviously a family of strong faith. About two weeks after the funeral, I stayed behind at the end of Sunday school as my classmates filed out of the classroom.

"Mrs. Adams," I asked. "Can people in heaven look down and see us from up there?"

I remember her answer more for its reassuring and kind tone than for what she actually said.

"Oh Jeff, I know your parents can see you right now and are so proud of you and will always be watching over you."

That's what I needed to hear. I had been scared about the future, but hearing that my parents still could see me and loved me put my twelve-year-old heart at ease. I guess I was looking for some connection. We had all just been abandoned abruptly and I guess you just figure out ways to cope with the situation.

I made it through the seventh grade. We all did, with a lot of help from some wonderful people. Aunt Agnes moved in with us guys; Uncle Clifford, John, Jim and me. Julie and Jerene went to live with Uncle Ralph and Aunt Marie Ann in Milwaukee. The summer break from school always provided a welcome mix of hard work in the fields, lazy days at the river, and a lot of fun with my friends. But this year, as the cries of "School's out!" faded and I rode the bus home, I had no idea what this summer would be like or even if I would ever go back to my school.

I was about to find out.

CHAPTER THREE

Now What?

Nobody talked about it.

My siblings and I had just lost our parents, yet nobody really sat down to listen to us and help process what happened. About the only thing I remember anyone saying about our loss occurred at the funeral home. And then it was stuff a seventh grader really didn't want to hear, much less understand.

But I do remember something someone told me. "I guess God needed your parents with Him more than we did." Sounds kind of mean, but when I thought about it that way, for some reason it made me understand and not be mad at God. Of course, now that I'm older, I see that may not be the most Biblically sound way to look at things, but it made sense to me. But beyond that, no adult sat down and talked with me about how I felt, or asked what questions or worries I had. In today's terminology, I never really processed what had just happened. None of us did. But back then nobody really processed anything. You just went on with your life.

So I returned to being the talkative kid who was an aspiring class clown. I kept things lively in the classroom, flirted with the girls, and probably cranked things up a notch or two just to show everyone I was still me—still normal. Because in the seventh grade, you just try to fit in. Which is why it didn't bother me at all that most of my teachers didn't say anything to me about the loss I had just suffered. It was pretty much business as usual, except for one teacher. Like I said, I was pretty talkative in class and not above disrupting it once in a while for laughs. I guess I pushed the limits of my English teacher because just before the end of the school year, he brought the hammer down on me pretty hard.

"Look, Olson," he practically screamed as he grabbed me by the arm. "I've gone pretty easy on you because of all you've been through, but I've had it up to here with your smart-mouth comments. Maybe a thousand-word essay on the eight parts of speech will help you remember to keep your mouth shut in class. Have it on my desk by tomorrow morning!"

That not only got my attention, but since then I've never had a problem with the eight parts of speech.

Other than that, hardly any teachers or adults ever said anything to me about the accident. No pats on the back or "hang in there" from anyone, which was fine by me. I just wanted to fit in. Or maybe I was just in what we call today denial. Who knows? Maybe all those adults were wise enough to know that singling me out for special attention is exactly what a seventh-grader doesn't need. Yet every now and then something would jar me back to reality, reminding me that I *was* different. I didn't have a mom or dad like everyone else in school. Like the time in chorus class. We were singing a Bob Dylan tune: "Blowing in the Wind." This was the Sixties when Dylan was hugely popular, so the chorus teacher probably thought we'd take music more seriously if we sang the songs we heard on the radio. But then we got to the verse, "How many deaths will it take 'til we know, that too many people have died?" Those words hit me like a freight train. Death. Just that word alone was enough to suck all the oxygen out of the room. The instant we sang that verse, I felt everyone's eyes locked on me. Whether they really were staring at me or not didn't matter. As far as I was concerned, the entire school was pointing a finger at me, reminding me that I was different. Weird thoughts, but I guess that happens when you don't make space to process painful things.

On the other hand, it's not like no one cared. They just didn't express it so much in words, and I'll never forget the time our neighbors told us just how much they cared about my family without saying a single word.

Farm life is pretty laid back and predictable for most of the year. But on two occasions, it becomes a desperate race against time and the elements: planting and harvest. In the spring, you have a small window of time in which to till the soil and plant your crops. It's like a square dance where Mother Nature is the caller. Back in the '60s, the way we did it was different than the way they do it today. But, once it's warm enough and the soil has dried out from the snowmelt, you would go over it with a plow, then a disc, and often with yet another piece of tillage equipment to rake it smooth. Then the actual planting begins. But every step of this dance can stumble to a halt with a period of heavy rain—a setback that can affect how the crops grow and whether or not you'll have enough at harvest time. Once planting season started, Dad and Uncle Clifford spent most of their time on the tractors, trying to get everything in the ground before a thunderstorm interrupted. It's not unusual to drive by Iowa farms after dark and see the tractor lights piercing the night.

Even though I was only twelve years old, now and then it crossed my mind: "How are we gonna get the planting done without Dad?" He was the field general who coordinated everything, but he was gone. No way could Uncle Clifford do it alone, and even though we had all driven tractors, the three of us boys weren't yet skilled enough to join in with the planting.

One beautiful April afternoon, I was ruminating on these things as I rode the bus home. Our bus stop offered a wide panoramic view of our entire farm, and as I stepped off the bus, I could hardly believe my eyes when I look out across the fields. Imagine how I felt as I looked out at a half dozen tractors crisscrossing the fields. John Deere. Allis Chalmers. Farmall. Massey Ferguson. And just one solitary Oliver. Some pulled huge plows that turned over the black soil, infusing the air with a pleasing earthy aroma. Others followed pulling discs that broke up the clumps and smoothed the fields. Still others crept behind with corn planters and wheat drills, dropping the precious seeds into the earth. My parents' friends and our neighbors weren't just lending a hand. Not just dropping off flowers and bringing over meals, but these folks were all taking time out of their busy planting schedules and working our fields – giving both hands – going above and beyond the call of duty. That picture never left me. Something told me it was going to be alright. I felt so good that Uncle Clifford was getting help. I couldn't have known it at the time, but seeing so many people come together for a cause would shape my own efforts to help others.

. . . our neighbors weren't just lending a hand . . .

By the end of the school year, it was decided that we would all go live with my aunt and uncle—Ralph and Marie Ann Seifert—in Wisconsin. Which meant I wouldn't be coming back to Waukon Junior High. So a bunch of parents got together and threw a big farewell party for us. It was great. We had cake, ice cream, and games. And the next day, we were gone. Off to the big city of Milwaukee in Uncle Ralph's big blue station wagon. I don't think any of us three boys wanted to go, but this was the way it was going to be. As fortune would have it, a week later, we were back on the farm, and nothing could have made me happier. This was my home. A place I understood. A place of pain, yes, but of comfort as well.

It turned out that Uncle Clifford needed help with the day-to-day business of running the farm. He was sixty-five years old and previously had always had my dad and us boys to help with the chores. Thanks to our neighbors, the crops were in, but they had their own chores to do, and no one expected them to stop by every day to help Uncle Clifford. He discovered real fast that he just couldn't handle it all by himself and put out a distress call to Uncle Ralph: "Sure would be good to have the boys here helping with the farm!"

Of course, we were thrilled. Nothing against my aunt and uncle, but we didn't want to live in Milwaukee. We were farm kids, and the city seemed like a foreign country to us. To be honest, when I first learned of this plan to send us to Milwaukee, I was scared. It just seemed so big and different—and unfair. None of the grownups asked us what *we* wanted to do. They just made an arbitrary decision. At least that's what I thought. I hadn't known then, nor could I have, that my dad and Uncle Ralph had earlier made a pact to take in each other's kids if anything happened to either of them. Uncle Ralph was just honoring the commitment he had made to my dad. Still, I was overjoyed that we would have at least one more summer on the family farm.

Looking back, those three summer months on the farm served as a perfect transition from one stage of my life to the next. Uncle Clifford and Dad had a sister, Aunt Agnes, who moved in with us. She was a widow and was more than happy to take care of all the domestic chores. So we had some semblance of a family for the summer.

During the day I helped with chores, which kept me occupied and made the hours speed by. Then in the evening, I could do pretty much anything I wanted. My girlfriend lived about a mile away, so we would bike together or just sit under a tree and talk. I also had my woods. If they had always offered me a comforting diversion from everyday life before, they became especially life-bringing to me as a kid who had just lost his parents and was facing an uncertain future. There were moments of joy that were a reprieve from the pain. That was also the summer of the moon landing. When I wasn't with my girlfriend, I was in the woods. Climbing trees. Building forts. Creating mini-lakes by damming up the stream. The woods became my refuge, a place where I could be myself and not worry about what anyone thought about me. Someone had given me a harmonica, and that summer I taught myself how to play it in those woods. With no one around to listen, who cared if I made mistakes?

Working on the farm in the fresh country air, hanging out with friends in the evenings, tromping through the woods—it really doesn't get much better than this. But it did. It seemed like at least once a week neighbors would invite us to their place for a picnic, and you haven't lived until you've experienced an Iowa farm family's picnic. Hamburgers and hot dogs on the grill, deviled-eggs, potato salad, home-made biscuits, juicy tomatoes, fresh corn on the cob, and crisp lettuce picked fresh from the garden, all washed down with ice cold tea or lemonade. Then often finished off with a fresh-baked dessert of some kind. Rhubarb if you're lucky!

. . . it was time to leave the farm for good.

Late in August I was finishing up my chores when I saw it. The big blue station wagon kicking up a cloud of dust as it rumbled up our lane. Something twisted inside my stomach as I turned and headed for the house. I knew the arrival of Aunt Marie Ann meant only one thing: it was time to leave the farm for good. I joined my brothers inside, packing whatever we could fit into the boxes Uncle Clifford gave us. We didn't say much. We didn't have to.

I felt like crying, but held back the tears because that's what boys are taught to do. But the emotions snaked through my young psyche like an unwelcome intruder. Sure, I was sad to be leaving the only home I had ever known, leaving behind my friends as well as a way of life I knew would change. But I was also scared. I'd heard that the new school I would be attending was huge.

Would I be able to make new friends? Would kids make fun of me because I came from the farm? It didn't help that as we headed the car back toward the highway, Johnny Cash was singing "A Boy Named Sue" on the radio. For all I knew, I would be just as different as the boy named Sue when I got to Milwaukee.

Three and a half hours later, we pulled into Uncle Ralph's driveway. The farm boy was now a city boy.

And did he ever have a lot to learn.

CHAPTER 4

Starting Over

We pulled into Uncle Ralph's driveway Sunday afternoon and started school the next day. Over the summer, Ralph had put up a couple of walls in the corner of his basement, added some bunk beds, dressers, and desks. That would be our bedroom, which was fine with us. Back on the farm my two sisters shared a room, just as I did with my brothers. Without much fanfare, we carried our clothes down the stairs of my aunt and uncle's ranch house, claimed a bed, and unpacked. Pretty soon it was time for supper, and then a little later, we were climbing into our beds. Just as I reached to shut off the lights, I heard Uncle Ralph coming down the stairs. He entered our room and sat on the edge of John's bed.

"Boys," he began. "I know you're probably a little worried about starting out in a new school tomorrow. It won't be easy. But you'll make it, and if you have any problems just let me know."

We all nodded and mumbled the kinds of things you're supposed to say when you're getting a pep talk like this.

"Now I know you're friends with Kathy next door, but you really need to make some good guy friends. Because the guys will be there for you the rest of your lives. So make some guy friends, okay?" He paused and looked down at his shoes as if he was searching for the right words. "Um, I'm glad you're here, boys."

And then he got up and left.

The actual name of the suburb that was our new home was Brookfield. And even though we were the new kids on the block, we were actually pretty familiar with the neighborhood because we had visited Uncle Ralph and Aunt Marie Ann many times. Of course, Mom and Dad were always with us, so it was strange at first to be there on our own. But like my uncle had said, over the years we had gotten to know Kathy, the girl next door, and her family. They had an above-ground swimming pool that we enjoyed on our summer visits.

The next morning, we got up, put on our school clothes, ate a good breakfast, and headed out the door; and there was Kathy waiting for us. I'm sure we would have made it that first day without Kathy, but she became a guardian angel to us as she walked us to the bus stop and then at school showed us where to go. Then after school she waited for us so that we knew which bus to get on for the ride back home. Kathy and I were both in the eighth grade, and somehow I had never noticed before how pretty she was. It wasn't long before I had a new girlfriend.

We survived our first day and over a very large dinner table recounted all that had happened. Mind you, Ralph and Marie Ann had just seen their family grow from three kids to eight, with kids in elementary school, middle school, and high school. Aunt Marie Ann was a trooper. Every morning she presided over three shifts of breakfast, ushering each shift out the door as the next one sat down at the table, all while WEMP-AM played in the background. It was literally a three-ring circus and a far cry from what we had experienced back at the farm. It turned out that one of my new friends, Scott Dorsey, was the son of Joe Dorsey, the morning drive-time disc jockey, which made it even cooler when I heard him on the radio, especially after I got a chance to meet him. Big-city disc jockeys were celebrities back then, especially to a kid from Harper's Ferry.

That first year in Brookfield was something of a blur. To be honest, I think I spent most of the year in a state of low-grade shock. I did okay on my grades. I didn't cause any problems for my teachers. I don't know if this helped or not, but no one besides Kathy knew why we had moved; knew that we were orphans. To my classmates, I was just another new kid.

I thought about my parents all the time, but especially when I saw other kids with their parents. And that was tough. Uncle Ralph and Aunt Marie Ann would, of course, attend all the school functions as a parent, but I knew they weren't my real parents. And I wished that Mom and Dad could have been there instead of them.

There was one day during the fall of that first year in school that I came bursting through the front door at the end of the day, with quite a bit more enthusiasm than normal. I had gotten to know a guy in school who said his dad could get tickets to the Green Bay Packers game. Back then, they played half their games in Milwaukee and the other half at Lambeau Field in Green Bay. He was talking on and on about

Any time I saw a family together, my heart dropped like a falling leaf.

how we would be able to meet some of the players and sit with the newspaper guys. I was floating I was so excited. I burst through that door and yelled, "Mom! I might be able to go to a Packers game and meet some of the players!" Right after I said it, I realized what I had said. It felt weird. It felt sad. I remember feeling a little awkward. It would have been a good chance for some processing, but Aunt Marie Ann and I just rolled on through and neither one of us even mentioned it. I just wished I could have had some more time with Mom and Dad.

I'm sure Aunt Marie Ann wished the same thing. She was dealing with the loss of her best friend and sister. This was hard for everyone. Any time I saw a family together, my heart dropped like a falling leaf. I really missed my mom and dad. I'm sure my brothers did too, but we never talked about it. No one did. Basically, that first year we all tried to figure out how to live together. How eight kids would take turns in the bathroom. How we would share the chores, which had nothing to do with hay or pigs or tractors. My brothers and I had to learn how to be city kids; and my cousins, Sue, Lori, and Sandy, who had lost their favorite aunt and uncle, had to learn how to share their parents with us, which was no small sacrifice. And for the most part, it all seemed to work pretty well.

For almost the entire school year, I rode up front on the school bus with Kathy. At first, she was my security blanket, insulating me from the terror of having to try and blend into a new group of kids. And later, because we had made that unspoken transition from friends, to really good friends, to "you wanna go to the dance with me" friends. But that relationship had its downside, especially in light of my uncle's admonition to make some guy friends. While I rode with Kathy up front, all the guys in my neighborhood rode in the back of the bus, and there was a certain mystique about the boys in the back of the bus. I had gotten to know them in school and they were nice guys and they were the cool guys, and naturally I wanted to be cool too. As long as I sat up front with a girl...well, it was nice, but it wasn't, if you know what I mean.

Finally, on about the second to the last day of school, I mustered up as much courage as I could and walked to the back of the bus. I remember one of them saying, "What took you so long?" I can't for the life of me understand why it took me so long, other than the fact that I felt so different, so conspicuous in needing my guardian angel. Being accepted by the guys pretty much completed the transition from new kid to regular kid, but it also had its downside.

I suppose if my parents had still been alive and I was living on the farm, I would have eventually discovered cigarettes and beer, but probably not until much later. But as I entered the ninth grade, my new guy friends started smoking and doing a little drinking, which meant, of course, that I did too. My uncle soon discovered my extra-curricular activities and did his best to rein me in. But I hadn't just started smoking and drinking, I started to give him a little attitude too. My friends weren't really bad guys, just pretty typical suburban boys who didn't have a barn or a woodlot or gut-busting chores to simmer their desire for fun.

To put it mildly, about halfway through the ninth grade, I became a bit of a handful. Keep in mind, however, that from the sixth grade until the tenth grade, I had been to five different schools. And you sort of had to prove your mettle at each new school, especially a farm kid in the affluent suburb of Brookfield. I mean a guy has to try to fit in, right?

One of my buddies, Bob Gesell, got to go to New York City with his family during ninth grade, and when he came back, he brought a supply of "dirty novels." Tame by today's standard, and without any pictures, they were graphic enough to grab my attention. One day in science class, I pushed my teacher, Mr. Farragher, to the limit and he sent me back to the work room attached to our classroom. Sort of a time out. I pulled out my edgy, irresistible book and stuck it inside my science book and started reading. A few minutes later Mr. Farragher abruptly entered the room and immediately saw what was going on. That led to a trip to the principal's office, which resulted in a call home. Nothing like going through the whole day of school just knowing that when you get home, there was going to be a discussion.

My uncle worked out of an office in the basement, adjacent to our bedroom. I got home from school and walked past his office to our bedroom, trying not to draw too much attention to my presence, only to hear him call my name.

"Jeff, can you come in here a minute?"

I slouched into a chair across from his desk as he recounted his call from the principal, and my response pretty much summed up my attitude at the time.

"So what," I shrugged. "Who even cares?"

That was the first and only time my uncle laid a hand on me as he hopped up from his desk, grabbed my arm, and pulled me close to his face.

"Look, we've got nine people in this house going in one direction, and you're heading in another direction," he began. "I know you've had a tough time losing your mom and dad, but you know something? You can feel sorry for yourself for as long as you want and you know what? For a little while, a lot of other people will feel sorry for you too. But after a while, they're not going to care and soon you'll be the only one feeling sorry for yourself. So you can shape up and quit feeling sorry for yourself and start moving in the right direction."

I was walking around with a chip on my shoulder . . .

It was exactly what I needed. He was right. I *was* walking around with a chip on my shoulder, feeling "poor me," and not caring what my actions did to myself or others. He got my attention, and I'm grateful to this day that he did. I can't say that I did an abrupt about face, but I started to let go of those feelings of self-pity and began to try a little harder to pull my weight in this blended family I'd suddenly found myself in.

Several years later, my uncle told me, "Most kids from the time they're born until they're twelve years old, they develop this well of love with their parents. From the time they're thirteen until the time they're twenty, they use it all up."

As an uncle, Ralph was my favorite. On the farm, we always looked forward to his visits. He'd play football with us and convinced us all that we should be Green Bay Packers fans. But as a father, we clashed. Maybe that's because he got me when I was thirteen. He did the best he could, but he had no well to draw from.

CHAPTER 5

Adrift in College

Somehow I made it through high school. I partied a lot. Goofed off in class. Went to church on Sundays. Drove Uncle Ralph nuts. And scraped by with grades that usually ranged between a 3.0 and 3.5, but not really hitting my potential. I don't think I ever questioned whether or not I would go to college. With my grades, I wasn't a shoo-in, but I knew I would go somewhere. Whatever happened, however, I had a clear signal that it was time to move on. Uncle Ralph and Aunt Marie Ann gave me a suitcase for my high-school graduation present.

In those days, your parents didn't drive you all over the country for college visits. I'd been to Luther College in Iowa many times because so many of my family members attended there, but I had no interest in following in their footsteps and the price was out of my range. So when it came time for me to choose, I did pretty much what I had done all through high school. I followed the crowd, and that meant I would apply to the University of Wisconsin in Madison. I hadn't filled out any other applications and I was just hoping for the best. So you can imagine how ecstatic I was when I go that letter in the mail: "Welcome to the University of Wisconsin." In just three short months I would be heading to Madison, Wisconsin, with a lot of my friends.

Of course, getting accepted into a college and paying for it are two different things. My aunt and uncle weren't able to help out much, and I don't think any of us expected them to. I would have to earn my way, which wasn't really a problem for me. Ever since junior high school, I had found ways to earn money, usually through lawn jobs. I can't say I had developed the discipline of saving my money, but at least I learned that if I wanted something, I had to work for it—a quality that would be put to good use the rest of my life.

Unlike today, back then most kids could earn enough with a good summer job to pay for the next year's college. During my junior and senior years, I had a part-time job with Kohl's Bakery. We made all the baked goods for the Kohl's food stores. Luckily, I was able to work full-time during the summer. If that name sounds familiar it's because Max Kohl, who started the bakery, eventually built it into a chain of sixty-three grocery stores that eventually became the department store chain bearing his name.

Talk about a "cake" summer job. For one thing, I spent my shift inside the freezer, and if you've ever experienced summer in the Midwest you know why that's considered a perk. But I also handled cake all day. Actually cakes and tortes and other pastries. Day in and day out I would pull on a sweatshirt and don some gloves and begin packing up the pastries in boxes. Then, I would load up the truck waiting at the dock to deliver these sweet treasures all over southeast Wisconsin and Illinois.

And I learned to save.

From the very first week, I took $100 from my paycheck and deposited it into a saving account. By the end of the summer I had $1,200 in savings, which was just enough to pay my tuition for the year. I also worked lawn jobs on the weekends, earning $5 for every lawn I mowed, which put enough money in my pocket to have some fun while I was at college. Room and board, of course, was extra, and here's where Uncle Ralph entered the college expense picture. Apparently, there was a settlement from the insurance company related to the accident that took my parents' lives. Ralph had set up savings accounts for each of us kids, depositing the settlement equally between us. He also informed me that I would now be getting a $110-per-month Social Security check, so between my own hard work and these two surprise benefits, I was able to pay my own way through college. It wasn't easy, but paying my own way taught me how to get the most out of a little.

I'd like to say I entered the University of Wisconsin with dreams of starting my career. But as far as I was concerned, college was party time, and Wisconsin had the reputation of being a huge party school. Most of my high school buddies were all there and we took advantage of every opportunity to have fun. I had no idea what I was going to do if and when I earned my degree. Heck, I changed majors almost as often as I changed my clothes. As far as my grades went, I did okay,

. . . paying my own way taught me how to get the most out of a little . . .

but you couldn't have called me a serious student. I learned the fine art of cramming—pulling all-nighters before exams, doing pretty well on the test, but forgetting most of what was on that test the next day.

As far as my faith was concerned, I followed the examples of just about everyone that I knew in college. I immediately quit going to church, and all of that God stuff moved to the back of my mind. In high school I attended regularly with the rest of my siblings and cousins and went through Confirmation. But that all stopped the minute I arrived in Madison. If in high school I held onto a belief in God, I let go of that in college. Keep in mind, this was right at the end of the Vietnam War and our society was going through a lot of changes. Our nation was undergoing a huge social upheaval from Watergate and the resignation of President Nixon, to Kent State and campus protests across the country. "Sex, drugs, and rock and roll" was more than just a colloquialism. From my perspective, it was robustly lived out by nearly every college student in America. So when the prevailing attitude about religion at Wisconsin was that God is dead or at least irrelevant, that seemed to fit in with the lifestyle I was living. As I look back, I don't think I ever stopped believing in God or all things I'd been taught from childhood, but you certainly wouldn't have called me a practicing Christian.

If I had to come up with one word to describe me during that first year in college, it would be aimless. I'm sure some of that came from never really coming to terms with the loss of my parents. Partying and not taking life real seriously became another way of not talking about it. In today's language, you would call it anesthetizing the pain. But a lot of it was just my own selfish and perhaps immature desire to have a lot of fun. In the back of my mind I may have been wondering what I would do in the future, but it must have been tucked way back there because I honestly don't remember ever thinking much about a career. I'm not proud of this, but about all I cared about that year was girls and getting high. If the party prospects for the weekend weren't all that great on campus, I'd drive back home to Milwaukee where I still had my girlfriend and a lot of other friends who knew how to have a good time.

Even though I think Uncle Ralph was glad to see me head off to college, he still did his best to provide the guidance that I desperately needed. By then, he knew all about my partying, and on one of my trips back to hang out with my girlfriend and friends, he sat me down late one night and gave it to me straight.

"Jeff, you can't possibly do well in college with all the partying you're doing," he began. "You've got to stop. And you need to quit coming back here. You've got to stay on campus, study instead of party, and think about what you want to do with the rest of your life."

You think I paid attention? I let his words go in one ear and out the other. Think about the rest of my life? I thought only as far ahead as the next party. The rest of my life could wait. I was having way too much fun. And amazingly, I was doing okay in my classes. A lot of freshmen flunk out their first semester—I think colleges even plan for a certain percentage to pay their tuition and then head home for good shortly after the deadline to get a refund. But between my cramming and probably taking those intro classes, I finished my first semester hovering around a 2.75 grade point average. So you think I changed my ways at all as I began my second semester? Hardly, but I did need to start thinking about how I was going to spend the upcoming summer.

I thought only as far ahead as the next party.

Sometime in March of my freshman year, my roommate, John Dinsmore, told me about a company that was on campus recruiting students for summer work. When he told me the job involved going door-to-door selling books, I laughed it off. Then when he said he had signed up, I really let him have it.

"I can just see you going door-to-door in some godforsaken city trying to sell books to little old ladies!"

Yet no matter how much I made fun of him, he kept telling me I should look into it, and I guess he just wore me down. I decided to go to the company's next recruiting meeting just to check it out. I was pretty sure I could get my old job back at Kohl's bakery, but John kept saying I could make a lot more money selling books. I sat in the back of the room as a representative from the company, Southwestern, explained how we would be assigned to a city somewhere in the United States, that we would start early in the morning and go door-to-door until almost dark. I was ready to bolt. But then he explained that we would get forty percent of each sale, and I started doing the math in my head. John was right. I wouldn't have to sell that many books to make more than I could make at the bakery. Still, I wasn't ready to commit. Even though Southwestern would provide training, I didn't think of myself as a salesman and wasn't sure I wanted to learn the ropes.

A couple of weeks after I attended the meeting, I drove home for Easter. After church and a big Easter dinner, I told Uncle Ralph about the sales job and his first question was how much they would pay me. When I told him I would get forty percent of every sale, he repeated almost verbatim what John had told me.

"Why, you only have to sell two or three books a day at that rate," he affirmed. "I think you ought to give it a try."

I couldn't have known it at the time, but looking back, I think there was another reason Uncle Ralph encouraged me to become a traveling book salesman. I'd be out of his hair all summer. Something tells me that he kind of got used to me not being around, and he liked it. Oh, how I love that man!

As I drove back to Madison, I thought long and hard about the job. I wasn't too thrilled about going door to door, but at least I'd get a chance to see part of the country I hadn't seen before. I had no idea where they would assign me, but I was pretty sure it would be more exciting than Milwaukee. And I'd probably find some guys to party with. By the time I got back to my dorm room, I had made up my mind. The next day I met with the recruiter from Southwestern and signed up for the summer.

That might have been the first smart decision I had made thus far in my young life.

CHAPTER 6

Door to Door . . . and More

Between classes I walked across campus to the Holt Commons, where I met Dick Justmann. A sophomore who spent the previous summer selling books for Southwestern and returned to campus as their student manager for the university. His primary role was to recruit additional students to join the team, but I had already made up my mind that this job had everything I wanted: travel, fun, and the opportunity to make a lot of money. He went through his recruiting notebook with me, explaining what I had already learned from my roommate, John. As soon as he finished I think I surprised him with my response.

"Sign me up!"

I guess it usually took a little convincing to recruit new salesmen, but I was ready. He gave me a form that I had to fill out and have co-signed by my uncle. In essence, it was a letter of credit that allowed me to borrow money from Southwestern to purchase their books at a wholesale price. I made a quick trip back to Milwaukee to get my uncle's signature, raced back to campus, turned in my form, and officially became a salesman for Southwestern—one of about thirty from the University of Wisconsin. I attended a few more meetings to learn the ins and outs of selling, record keeping, and the importance of good discipline—you can't make a sale if you're sleeping in or quitting early. At one of these meetings, I met Dick's boss, our Sales Manager, Ashoke Menon. He had worked in the program for about five years and the first time he met me he said, "Hey JT! Dick told me about you. Said you were a pretty sharp guy!"

. . . you can't make a sale if you're sleeping in or quitting early.

Now I know he was being an encourager, but honestly, that was the first time anyone had told me I was sharp. Whether or not that statement was true doesn't matter, but it did something inside me. It was also the first time an adult called me JT. It was a nickname that I had gotten in high school and mostly just used by my close friends. One of the forms I filled out had a space for a nickname and that's all I could come up with. I guess it stuck. It all made me feel special. I began to like these guys. It soon became clear that this wasn't going to be a walk in the park, but something about that even made me more determined to stick with it. Of course, I had a lot of my friends telling me I was crazy, but I stuck with my decision.

As soon as exams were over, we all headed for Nashville for a week of even more intense training. I didn't have a car, so hitched a ride with a carload of other recruits and we drove non-stop from Madison to the Music City where, as directed by Southwestern, we checked into the Admiral Benbow Hotel. Or I should say crammed into the hotel because eight of us shared a room with four double beds.

The training was as thorough as it was intense. For the next five days we were supposed to report to the War Memorial Building at 7:30 a.m. to learn what it takes to become great salesmen. In retrospect, it's probably one of the greatest sales training programs in the country, but I walked into that first session with only one goal: to show everyone how I was too cool for this and disdained the whole rah-rah-rah of sales training. Most of my group from Wisconsin had the same goal. So when everyone else stood up and cheered whenever a speaker challenged us, we just sat there practically dripping with cynicism. Apparently, someone noticed because later that night one of the student managers from another group came into our hotel room.

"Listen guys, I know you think you're above all this, but let me tell you something," he began. "You better start taking this seriously because when you go out to sell books next week, if you don't develop some enthusiasm, you're not gonna make it!"

And that forty percent of nothing is nothing.

We may have been a motley crew, but we weren't stupid. It dawned on me that in a few days I would find myself somewhere in the U.S. trying to convince people to buy what I'm selling. And that forty percent of nothing is nothing. I'd given up a sure thing at Kohl's Bakery and in the process, made my girlfriend mad because I would be gone all summer. Maybe I should start paying attention.

But this guy wasn't done with us.

"When you first signed up, you committed to three things," he continued. "To work hard, study hard, and be teachable. Well guess what. You're not being teachable when you just sit there looking like you know it all."

And he was right. When he recruited me, Dick Justmann, asked me those three questions. Could I work hard? Could I study hard? Am I teachable? I assured him I was, but having this student manager from another team confront us was like getting smacked up the side of the head with the truth. But to his credit, he didn't leave it at that, probably knowing that you can't scold someone into action. You need to lead, and that's exactly what he did.

"Let me give you a little example that will help you this summer," he explained. And then he began quietly and slowly repeating, "If you act enthusiastic, you become enthusiastic. If you act enthusiastic, you become enthusiastic."

Each time he repeated that phrase, his voice got a little louder, his cadence faster. And after about the fourth or fifth time, he stood up and motioned for us to join him. At first, we sort of mumbled our way through his little mantra, a little embarrassed and sheepish. But he kept at it, getting louder and louder, jumping up and down and patting us on our backs. It took about two minutes before we were jumping around with him and shouting, "IF YOU ACT ENTHUSIASTIC, YOU BECOME ENTHUSIASTIC!"

. . . you can't scold someone into action. You need to lead . . .

He didn't make us do anything. He just led by example, and by the time we were done I realized, "This guy's right. If I act enthusiastic, I'll become enthusiastic." It's one of the most important life lessons I've ever learned; one that has gotten me through a lot of tough times. Simple? Yes, but so true, and from that moment I was all in. I realized for the first time in my life that I'm in charge of my attitude, not someone else. What a difference that made for all of us.

The next day at sales training, we cheered along with everyone else. Maybe even louder than the others. By the end of the week I had lost my voice, and not just from the cheering. I joined in on all the discussions and even kept at it back at the hotel after our training was done for the day. If I saw anyone lagging, I'd do my best to encourage them. We even came up with our own ditty, "I'm alert, alive, friendly, cordial, firm, enthusiastic!" Again, this may sound simplistic, but it was a way to boost our confidence. If you're not confident you're going to have a difficult time walking up to that door, and the moment was approaching when we would learn where we would be spending the summer. The folks at Southwestern wanted to fully equip us to succeed, and by the time I got my assignment, I *knew* I was going to be a great salesman.

Thursday after Sales School was finished for the day, my team of about twenty students learned that we would be selling books in Los Angeles. Back when we were recruited, they explained that once we got our assignments, we would be responsible for getting to our assigned terri-tory and finding a place to live. The next day a caravan of rag-tag cars found their way even-tually to Interstate 40, where for the next two days we subsisted on fast food and little sleep before rolling into the city. Our first order of business was to find a place to live.

I realized for the first time in my life that I'm in charge of my attitude, not someone else.

To cover Los Angeles, our team split into smaller groups of three or four. Our student leader basically pulled out a map and said, "Okay, you guys head to Inglewood, you guys to Downey, you guys to Montebello..." Keep in mind, this was before smartphones and GPS. Somehow we got to Alhambra and found a hotel that offered to put us up for $2 a night. Not exactly the Omni, but at least a place to sleep.

We hated it, but Southwestern had taught us how to use this to our advantage. They told us that the best way to get into a nicer living arrangement was to go out and start selling the very first day. Then after we make our sales presentation, we were to mention that we're looking for a place to live as we continue to work during the summer. The idea was that people would see that we were earnest about work and trustworthy and eventually we might find a family who had an extra room and wouldn't mind earning a little extra money from renting it out. Sure enough, it worked. After just two days in that hotel, John bounded into the room and announced, "Hey guys, we're outta here! I found a place."

What he found was basically a room about the size of small bedroom. Only one bed, with a mattress on the floor for whoever drew the shortest straw. But it was clean, and besides, all we needed was a place to sleep because we would be working from dawn to dusk. .

I'll never forget my first day. John had carved up the map of Alhambra into three zones, and to get to my zone I had to get up early and hitchhike down Atlantic Avenue to Main Street and then walk about a mile to Garfield Avenue. I left the hotel in the cool darkness of dawn but by the time I got to Garfield, the sun shone bright and warm. But it wasn't the heat that made my palms sweat. It was 7:55 a.m. We knew our hours by this little mantra: "I start knocking at 7:59, I don't stop knocking 'til half-past nine." I was so nervous I could almost hear my own heart beat above the din of the city.

At 7:59 sharp I knocked on the door of what I hoped would be my first customer. Nothing. I knocked again, and no one came to the door. You might say I was wading into it. I turned and looked across the street and saw a curtain move. Aha, I thought to myself as I grabbed my bag and ran up to that door and started knocking. A lady came to the window and shouted, "What you want?"

I explained that I was selling books and pulled one out so that she could see it, and she responded, "No speak English."

And I thought, this is going to be hard. Even then, Los Angeles was a city rich in diversity and it occurred to me that I would be trying to sell books to people who couldn't read them. Of course I was discouraged, but I remembered my training. "If you act enthusiastic, you will become enthusiastic." So undaunted, I kept at it and at my third call, I was invited inside.

Most of the books we sold were study guides, kid's books, and other resources aimed at helping young students do well in school. So when I got inside and saw that my customer had to school-aged children, my hopes soared. I went through my demonstration exactly as I had been trained and when it came time to close the deal I explained that the book she was interested in cost $17.35, plus tax and shipping, and then handed her the order form to sign.

My first sale, and it went exactly how my sales trainer said it would go. And there's nothing like making a sale to put a bounce in the step of a salesman. I approached the next house with confidence, and then next and the next and the next. That one sale made the day speed by until it was quitting time, "half-past nine." Thirteen and a half hours. But I was pumped. In addition to that one sale, I added three more before heading back to the hotel.

That summer in Los Angeles took its toll on an unusual number of our team—about half quit. It was tough. No matter how much they prepare you, no one likes facing rejection, but that's part of door-to-door selling. Honestly, people don't really slam the door in your face. Most of them politely reject you and you have to learn not to take it personal. But John and I made it, and despite the long hours and regular rejection, we had a blast. I earned enough to pay for the upcoming year of college, but I got a lot more than money out of my experience selling books for Southwestern. It all became clear to me at the very end of the summer and I believe laid the groundwork for many decisions that I would later make.

Our weekly Sunday sales meeting was over and Dick was driving John and I back to our place. I was in the front seat and was watching the city fly by me as we drove down Interstate 5. It was my last time to be with our team and I was thinking back on all that I had learned, all that I had accomplished. I had met face to face with about 3,000 people. That built my self-confidence like no factory job would have. I learned to handle myself in difficult situations, how to make people feel at ease with a stranger. I had also got some good lessons in hard work (as in about eighty hours a week) and perseverance, and I learned a lot about my strengths and weaknesses. On top of that, I felt really good about the books I had left with about 300 families. I had just experienced a life-changing summer and I'd made some money. To put it another way...I cleaned up my act a bit.

None of that would have happened if Dick Justmann hadn't recruited me, trained me, and put up with my "too cool" attitude. So I turned to Dick and said, "I just want you to know that I'm grateful for everything you've done for me this summer. I couldn't have done this without your help and guidance."

He just shrugged his shoulders, laughed and said, "Aw, that's okay. You could have done it without me, but you're welcome. It was my pleasure."

There was this silence as I turned back to watch the scenery go by, but the thought hit me, "He must feel great right now because I just thanked him for literally changing my life. If he doesn't, it just means I failed to convey how much he's influenced me. And then I thought, "I wonder what that must feel like? Wouldn't it be cool to have someone feel that way about me, someday?"

Originally I had no intention of coming back and putting myself through another difficult summer of book sales again. But this was the turning point where it dawned on me that maybe coming back, and bringing a team would be my chance to do that, have the same kind of impact on someone that Dick Justmann had on me.

Not to be overly dramatic, but working for Southwestern selling books that summer might have saved my life. It sure turned it around.

Just how much it would influence me I was about to find out.

CHAPTER 7

Life Is More Than Selling

Before I left to sell books that first summer, I told Aunt Marie Ann that I had one goal: to make enough money so that I could afford to buy a plane ticket and fly home. I did that and I earned enough to pay for my sophomore year at the University of Wisconsin. To say my self-esteem got a boost vastly understates just how good I felt about myself. For the first time in a long time, I was getting a lot of praise—from the members of our Los Angeles team, from our student manager, and from our sales manager. After we got back on campus, I learned that I was the top salesman for our team. That's a lot like being the best player on the 125th ranked team, but hey, it was more than I had ever done.

Unfortunately, I returned to my old partying habits. It was like I had to make up for lost time. When I was selling books, by the time I got back to our room all I could do was collapse on my bed. School was different because I could party with the best and still get decent grades. You would think some of the self-discipline

I learned, coupled with the affirmation I received for doing such a good job would have carried over into my academic pursuits.

Not exactly, but it did help with my work with Southwestern. I must have learned something, because I ended up recruiting thirteen people to come with me for my second summer. I was looking forward to helping them learn what I had learned my first summer. So when exams were over, the whole group from Madison headed to Nashville for Sales School.

Being in Sales School as a rookie and as a student manager with thirteen people looking to you for guidance are two different animals. It was fun and exciting, but it also made me realize how much I had to learn about leadership. On top of learning my own sales talks, I had to go to student manager meetings and spend individual time with each team member. I began to realize that if I was going to have an impact on someone, it wasn't going to come easy. This management stuff was hard work.

I began to realize that if I was going to have an impact on someone, it wasn't going to come easy.

After Sales School we headed to upstate New York. That summer in 1976 proved to be quite challenging. I was used to Los Angeles and this was upstate New York. I was used to walking and now I had a car. People were still basically the same. Most were nice, some were rude, and some bought books. The biggest challenge I had was staying on a schedule with my car. When you're walking and you get discouraged, you don't have a choice but to just go to the next door. When you have a car, all of a sudden there is an option. Unfortunately, there were a few times I lacked the mental toughness and chose poorly. Once you start cutting corners here and there, it can really mess you up.

We started with about thirty-nine people and ended up with thirteen finishing the summer. Our field leader even went home.

That's when my sales manager, Fred Prevost, called me up and said, "JT, you're in charge now." I had gotten to know Fred throughout the school year as he helped me recruit my team. To say I had a lot of respect for him would be an understatement. Something about that call put some fire in my belly and it gave me just a little more motivation and I finished the summer strong.

Financially, when it was over, I had made more than my first summer, but spent more. In the end I received a check for $52. That was a far cry from my first summer but I had nobody to blame but me. Somewhere I read that you learn more from your failures than you do your successes. I learned a lot that summer. Part of the reason for the tiny paycheck was that I had bought a car. Even though I sold more books, I had a lot of expenses, beginning with the purchase of that car. It wasn't exactly in great shape when I got it. Somewhere along the way, the gas tank sprang a leak, at the bottom. Yes, I learned a lot that summer. Probably the greatest personal lesson was the value of perseverance. No matter how tough it got, there was no way I was giving up.

At different points in the summer, especially towards the end, I had several guys come up and thank me for helping them get through the summer. That was a great feeling. Knowing that you had an impact on someone's life. From that point on I poured myself into Southwestern. I knew firsthand what happens when you go off schedule, so for the next few summers I led my teams with enthusiasm and it paid off. We weren't ever at the top when it came to sales, but we were headed in the right direction.

Throughout my time at Wisconsin, the pattern continued. Work like crazy selling books all summer, earn enough to pay for school, coast through my classes earning passing grades, and of course, party like there's no tomorrow. If you would have asked me about my faith at the time, I would have likely said I was a Christian, but in reality I had little room for God in my life. I didn't really rebel against my Christian upbringing; it just wasn't relevant to me.

Once during that first summer of selling, I landed in a lady's living room and quickly discovered she was real religious. I mean, a real Bible-thumping, holy-roller type. I wanted to sell her some books; she wanted to talk to me about Jesus. I fidgeted in that lady's house for more than an hour and still hadn't closed the deal. No matter what I said about the books, she brought the conversation back to Jesus. So when she asked me if I wanted to invite Jesus into my life, I thought, "Why not? I might even get a sale out of it." I know—not something to be proud of, but it worked.

I didn't really rebel against my Christian upbringing; it just wasn't relevant to me.

I made the sale, but I can't say I was all that sincere about following Jesus.

Then after my senior year, headed to the book field for one last summer, a senior vice-president of Southwestern took an interest in me. His name was Allen Clements, and he was something of a legend in the company. Sales School, which we all had to attend, was basically a combination of learning sales techniques and listening to motivational speeches. Allen's speech was one of my favorites—how his dad thought selling books was a waste of time and taunted him to find a better way to make something out of his life. I related to the way he refused to quit, eventually rising to a lucrative position in the company. So when he would drop by campus and spend some time with me, I couldn't believe my good fortune. Someone important is interested in *me*? It made me feel as if I mattered.

At the start of my fifth summer, on Thursday night of Sales School, just before we were to charge into the summer selling season, Allen picked me up in his car and drove way out into the country, talking the entire time about selling and the importance of staying on schedule. He also shared more stories of his own career and shared tips about selling and managing a team. I thought it was cool that a senior vice-president would send me off with his own personal words of encouragement, but then he pulled into a roadside park and shut off the motor, and the conversation quickly veered into another direction, one that caught me off guard.

"JT," he began, "What are you doing?"

"I don't know," I answered, not real sure where this conversation was going, "What do you mean?"

"I'm not talking about selling books. You're one of our best, and I know you're going to have a great summer. But life is more than selling books and making money. Where are you going with your life?"

But life is more than selling books and making money.

That really got my attention because I didn't have a clue. No one had ever asked me that before, and I sure wasn't sitting around pondering the deep questions of life.

"I'm not sure, Allen. I guess I've never thought much about my life."

And then in the most gentle yet compelling manner, he began explaining to me how God loved me and sent His Son to earth to die for my sins so that I could live a life of meaning and purpose. He quoted words from the Bible that I had heard as a kid in a Lutheran Sunday school, but on that night they connected. They made sense and helped me see myself in a new light. For the first time in my life I recognized my need for a Savior and made a conscious decision to invite Jesus into my life. I can't say that it had an immediate impact on my life—especially my lifestyle—but it planted a seed of conviction that life was more than having a good time or even making money. I had no idea what the future held for me, but I now realized that trusting God with my life was far better than going it alone. Throughout that summer, Allen periodically sent me notes to encourage me in my new-found faith, always with just the right Bible verse to assure me of God's love for me. I still had a long way to "grow" as a Christian, but to this day I'm grateful that Allen saw me as something more than just a student dealer of Southwestern. Towards the end of that fifth summer in Alabama, I got a call from Southwestern's headquarters in Nashville asking me to fly up there for a meeting. So I got on a plane out of Dothan, Alabama, and flew to Nashville, wondering all along what I had done. I didn't think they were going to fire me, but beyond that I didn't have a clue. Someone picked me up at the Nashville airport and we engaged in small talk until he dropped me off at Southwestern's offices. I found my way to the appointed office and when I walked in, two guys, Allen Clements and Fred Prevost, stood to greet me and almost immediately, the mystery behind this trip was solved.

If you don't do this now, you are always going to be asking yourself 'Could I have made it?'

"We'd like you to become a full-time sales manager."

My first response was, "No way." Even though I had experienced success both as a salesman and as a student leader, it was just too much hard work for my tastes. Also, I had seen sales managers—the position they were offering me—come and go. Turnover was high for a reason, and I wasn't about to jump into something that would burn me out in a year or two. But they persisted.

While I was thinking about this offer, one of my friends, Gary Atkinson, who was already a sales manager said, "If you don't do this now, you are always going to be asking yourself 'Could I have made it?' And I think you're going to regret that you didn't at least give it a try." Another factor was that I would be working with Fred Prevost again. We hadn't worked with each other since my second summer. We were a pretty good team and I knew I could learn a lot from that man. Not everyone gets a good mentor, but Fred was one of the best.

It all must have made sense, because I decided to take them up on their offer. But there was another reason I gave in. During my five years with Southwestern I had had four sales managers. I wanted to change that and give the students in Wisconsin someone they could count on. Every year when I returned to campus, I was so disappointed to learn that we had yet another new sales manager. Maybe this was so important to me because ever since my parents were killed I really didn't have anyone I could count on, outside of my family. I didn't know it at the time, but I was dealing with abandonment issues. So I made a promise to myself. I'm going to give the students some consistency—I'm going to do this for the next five years.

Even though I didn't have to, I returned to the field to sell with my team during my first year as sales manager. I thought it would help me build a better sales organization if the guys saw me out there selling right alongside them. I also needed the money, and for the first time ended up being one of the top salesman in the entire company that year. My team did well, too, which taught me an important lesson in leadership: lead by example. Let people see that you're willing to do what you're asking them to do. I knew that was the type of leader I responded to, and I wanted to do the same for others.

I also tried to set an example with my attitude. One summer I was taking part of my team to our assigned territory in North Carolina, and one of the guys, noticing that I was a little drowsy behind the wheel, offered to drive. Grateful for a break, I pulled over and let him drive. Earlier he had seen me slip the car in neutral when rolling down a hill—a not very smart way to try and save gas or your brakes. Only when he tried it, he shifted the car into reverse, bringing the car to a screeching halt, right there on the freeway, with all sorts of noises you don't want to hear coming from your transmission. My first thought was to reach over and slap him, but I wisely rejected that impulse. He was a squirrely kid and probably just trashed my car's transmission, but wringing his neck might be a bit much. And messy. Before I could unleash my anger in a fury of expletives, he practically broke down in tears.

"Oh no," he wailed. "What did I do?"

I quietly told him that he had mistakenly put the car in reverse which was why the car was not running and then asked him to try starting it back up. He gingerly turned the key and miracle of miracles, my little Pontiac started right up.

"We probably don't want to do that again, right?" I smiled, leaning back in my seat as if this sort of mishap occurred routinely.

That was all I said, and I could hardly believe my restraint. But I knew what it was like to get yelled at, and it usually only makes things worse. Trust me, I was tempted to scream at my team any number of times, but what kept me from blowing up is that I realized they're watching. Always watching to see what I would do. They're learning about life from me. If I wanted them to keep their cool when things go wrong, I had to model it for them. That's what being a leader is all about. That doesn't mean I always did the right thing. In fact, one of the best decisions I ever made involved violating a long-standing policy at Southwestern.

CHAPTER 8

Some Rules Are Made to Be Broken

Not too long after I graduated from the University of Wisconsin, I signed on to Southwestern full-time as a sales manager. I knew the risk of burnout that went with the job, but I was young, had enjoyed my years with them as a student salesman, and was eager to make my mark in the world. As a sales manager, I supported the efforts of about three sales groups, which included approximately one hundred student dealers. I moved to Nashville, rented an apartment, and got right to work managing a territory that included Wisconsin, Minnesota, Illinois, and Iowa. Even though the job required a lot of travel, as far as I was concerned, it was about as good as it gets. And it was about to get better.

One balmy day in May of 1982, my schedule called for me to interview new student sales prospects in Room 500—a suite— at a Howard Johnson's in Madison, Wisconsin. My home away from home. This was a part of my job that I really enjoyed—discovering talent. I wasn't much older than these prospects, and it was always fun getting to know them and discover the skills and attitudes they brought to the table.

I walked into the suite where ten nervous college students sat, but my eyes landed on one student in particular—an absolutely gorgeous young woman with an engaging personality. Now the purpose of these interviews was to recruit new sales people, so in a sense we were there to sell Southwestern. On this particular day, I had brought along one of my trainees and let him conduct the interview. Although he eventually became great at running these interviews, at this point he was quite green, and it showed. I sat toward the back of the room and groaned inwardly at his rookie efforts. Obviously, I wanted as many of these kids to sign up as possible, but I especially wanted that lovely freshman to join our team, figuring she could probably be very successful. I was worried that my trainee was practically guaranteeing that all ten of these prospects would leave without signing up. As it turned out, all but one did.

She was drop dead gorgeous and had a heart that matched.

The good-looking freshman girl from Sheboygan, Wisconsin.

During my tenure at Southwestern, I had noticed a lot of pretty girls who had signed up, but this girl, Sara Mattox, had something special about her that got my attention. She was drop dead gorgeous and had a heart that matched. Once she set out to her territory in Boston, she hit the ground running and did a great job, so naturally I wanted to sign her up again for the following season. Whenever you have a successful salesperson, it's in everyone's best interest to keep them on the team. That's one of the things I loved about Southwestern, if you helped a student do well, everyone wins. But I likely had other interests in mind when I flew to Boston for that group's Sunday meeting. I was meeting with all the students individually and she and I were set to meet in a coffee shop.

"I know why you're here," Sara began. "But I want you to know I've given this a lot of thought and no matter what you say, I've made up my mind, you can't change it."

My heart sunk, as I anticipated the next words that were about to come out of her mouth. I had fully expected her to say the work was too hard and that she never wanted to sell books again, which would mean I would probably never see her again. I braced myself as she broke into a broad smile.

"I wouldn't miss it for the world!"

You can imagine my relief at her response.

Sara returned to the university in the fall and almost immediately began recruiting other students for the following summer. Who wouldn't want to join this vivacious young woman? By springtime she had recruited twenty-four students, almost unheard of for a rookie student manager. But she was a natural, and it wasn't just her good looks that drew people to her. She was smart and funny, but also tough. And what made this so great for my group was that she recruited people just like herself.

Because Sara recruited so many students, I spent a lot more time with her than I did with other student managers. Most of the other students signed on only two or three recruits the entire year. Whenever they had a new recruit, I would show up to interview them and help explain what they would be doing. So at least twenty-four times during that year, I met with Sara and her recruit, and always after those meetings, she asked me to stick around to answer her questions. I know this may sound like an exaggeration, but she would literally sit on the floor at my feet, notebook in hand, as she peppered me with questions about selling and managing. She soaked up knowledge like a sponge and clearly wanted to excel as a student manager. Of course, I was happy to oblige.

To be perfectly honest, my interests as we went into that school year were strictly professional, but I couldn't help notice how attractive she was because hey, I'm a guy. But first and foremost, I was just thrilled to have such a capable student manager on my team and appreciated her desire to learn and improve. Besides, Southwestern frowned on sales managers dating their students for obvious reasons. If anything else was going on in her mind, I was unaware of it.

But not for long.

Toward the end of the second semester, things started to change. While it was clear that we both respected each other, we also began to like each other on a level beyond colleagues. I admired what she was doing, but I also found myself eagerly anticipating my campus visits just so I could see her again. As we would spend time together talking about selling books, the conversations often wandered into more personal territory so that for all practical purposes these "study sessions" became more like dates. So much so that during a pause in our casual conversation one evening in May, I took a big chance, leaned over, and gave her a kiss. I guess she wasn't too surprised because she held me close before we both stood up awkwardly. That meeting was over pretty quick and she headed back to her apartment. Neither of us talked about it, but I think we both knew that our relationship had changed in that wonderful embrace.

After she finished the spring semester, Sara left for the Washington DC area. Naturally, as a good sales manager, I organized my travel schedule to visit her team quite a bit that summer, and it wasn't long before others noticed my special interest in her budding sales career. Once people notice these things, it's hard to keep it a secret, though Sara and I did our best not to be real obvious about what was going on between us.

Eventually, word of our relationship got to my boss, Fred Prevost, who approached me about it. When he asked me if what he had heard was true, I had to be honest. I acknowledged that I was falling in love with Sara and assured him that I wasn't just playing around. Everyone knew that I dated a lot of women (outside of Southwestern), so I had a bit of a reputation in that department. But I had never had feelings for anyone like I had for Sara, and if I would have to choose between her and my job, I would have walked away from Southwestern in a heartbeat. Fortunately, Fred gave me his blessing, and that's when I began my own selling campaign: to convince Sara to become my wife.

Sara had grown up in a loving Christian home and gave her life to Christ while in high school. I knew she had strong feelings for me, especially at the beginning of our relationship. But she knew I dated around a lot and I think that conflicted with her values. After a while, she conveniently found excuses for not seeing me, and I began to think I might have blown it with her. That's when I realized I was truly in love with her, and I almost panicked at the thought of her spending the rest of her life with someone else. Somehow I convinced her to go out with me again, which got our relationship back on track. But that wasn't enough for me. I started talking to her about marriage and she was open to the idea but wasn't in any hurry. She wanted to finish college first, which was a real disappointment to me.

One night over a nice dinner I must have pressed my case pretty hard because Sara stopped me in the middle of a sentence.

"JT, why are you in such a hurry?!?"

I felt my chin quiver and my eyes well up with tears. Normally, I could glibly talk my way out of or into anything, but my answering was short and halting.

"I...don't...want...to...lose...you..."

Other than my parents and siblings, I had never loved anyone as much as I loved Sara. The thought of losing her hit me with nearly the same force that losing my parents did. I looked across the table as Sara reached for my hand, fearful that she would try to gently tell me what I didn't want to hear. Maybe she was just being nice by agreeing to see me again. Maybe she had met another guy and didn't have the courage to tell me. I braced myself as she began to softly speak.

"JT, I love you and will always be faithful to you. You don't ever have to worry about other men. There is only you."

But it wasn't other men I was afraid of losing her to. "I'm afraid..." I stammered, "of losing you..." and I blinked back tears as I finally said the words I'd never uttered to anyone else, "...the way I lost my mom and dad. Suddenly, and without warning, I was all alone. And I vowed to do everything in my power to protect myself so I would never feel that pain again."

But I realized, now I had a choice; a decision. And I was ready to trust God, again, and tell the woman I loved that I wanted to spend the rest of my life with her. Clearly, I had a lot to learn about the way God loved me, and He was using this woman to do it.

I was ecstatic and relieved. And I was determined to close the deal. A few days later I found just the right ring and devised a plan to formally ask for Sara's hand in marriage. After the rest of the students in my organization had left to go back to their campuses following a spring production meeting, Sara and I went for dinner at the resort restaurant. She thought it would be just another evening, but I knew what was coming.

We ordered drinks and then scanned our menus. Somehow I diverted her attention when the drinks arrived, deftly dropping the ring into her drink. I could hardly contain myself as she reached for her drink, then set it aside after a small sip. I tried not to focus on her glass as we enjoyed our dinner, but it drove me crazy that she wasn't finishing it. We finished our meal and were about to leave when she took one more sip of her drink and saw the ring.

Mission accomplished!

Even as we celebrated on the way to my car, we began planning our wedding. Or more accurately, Sara planned while I internally groused about all the time, money, and bother that go into a wedding. This was a big issue with me. It seems like all the emphasis in your classic bridal magazine is on weddings, not building a quality marriage. *My* plan was to be married to Sara forever, not to make sure the guys' tuxedos matched the girls' gowns. And trying to find a date that accommodated everyone's schedules just added to my misery.

After a few months, even Sara was beginning to see my point that the focus on a wedding can divert the focus from the relationship. We both were headed to a sales event in Reno, Nevada when I popped the *other* question: Why don't we just elope?

Which is exactly what we did. We found a minister who married us in a little park in Carson City and spent our honeymoon day driving around Lake Tahoe in a limousine. What a blast when the next day we were able to tell our colleagues that we were now husband and wife! Of course they were shocked, but thrilled for us, and we all celebrated with a big party back in Nashville a few weeks later.

We both decided that being married was more important than getting married.

I'm not saying this is how everyone should get married, but for us, it seemed like the right thing to do. We both decided that *being married* was more important than *getting* married. And that pulling off a huge wedding does not guarantee that anyone will *stay* married.

Besides, running off to Reno to get married would give us a great story to share with our kids.

That is, if we ever decided to have any.

CHAPTER 9

The Value of a Life

Something happens when you go to church every week. Once you begin hearing regularly from the word of God, it changes your outlook. You begin to see things in a new light, and nowhere was that more evident for me than on the issue of life itself.

When I was in high school, the Supreme Court ruled on a landmark case: Roe v. Wade. By a vote of 7-2, the highest court in the land granted women the right to have an abortion. I'm not proud to admit this, but I was one of those who applauded this decision because as a guy, it meant that if I got a girl pregnant, I was off the hook. She could just go to a clinic and legally terminate the pregnancy. That perspective seems to be overlooked in our culture today. It told men that they have little to no responsibility for their actions.

I'd like to claim that when I turned my life over to Christ I cleaned up my act, but the truth is I was still a pretty big party animal. But after I got married and we started going to church regularly, I began to see that I couldn't live for God on Sunday and go back to my wild ways the rest of the week. I learned that salvation was more than a way to stay out of hell; it was a relationship with a Savior who wanted the very best for me. As I began to read the Bible and pray and pay attention to sermons, I gradually began to change the way I lived. I developed a desire to honor and obey God, and as I grew spiritually my views on abortion radically changed. Instead of seeing it as a convenient way to avoid having an unwanted baby, I recognized it for what it was: taking the life of an innocent child. To me, "thou shalt not kill" meant I could not support the pro-choice position without disobeying God.

Sara, too, had gone through a similar transformation. Despite being raised in a wonderfully Christian family, she was somewhat neutral on the issue of abortion, though if forced to come down on one side or the other, she would have leaned toward the pro-choice movement. Ironically, her views on this topic were shaped by her overall conservative values. As she explains it, "All of the slogans resonated with my view of a limited role of government: 'If you don't want an abortion, don't have one,' 'Every child a wanted child,' and 'Don't legislate my body,' all of which would be true if we are talking about organs rather than a little child."

Even though I embraced a pro-life position, Sara kept her pro-choice view to herself until one day after we were married she acknowledged that she believed a woman should have the right to have an abortion. I sort of knew that, but it was one of those things we never talked about. So since she brought it up, I simply asked her to read Psalm 139 and to seek God's guidance. She knew I would love her regardless of her stand on this issue, yet I was confident that her trust in God was greater than her trust in a political ideology. My confidence was not unwarranted, for after she read, "For you created my inmost being; you knit me together in my mother's womb. I praise you because I am fearfully and wonderfully made….My frame was not hidden from you when I was made in the secret place, when I was woven together in the depths of the earth. Your eyes saw my unformed body; all the days ordained for me were written in your book before one of them came to be." (v. 13 - 16) She realized that God is the author of *all* life. We agreed at that time that if she ever got pregnant, our child would be given what every unborn child deserves: life.

Of course, by the time I arrived at that position, I was a happily married man devoted to Sara, so it's not like this change in my view would affect me personally. Instead of trying to avoid a pregnancy, we wanted to start a family. And in God's providence, though it was several years in the making, one hot August afternoon Sara finally returned from a doctor's appointment with the news: we're going to have a baby! We were both ecstatic. We had a nice place with a room picked out that would serve as a nursery. I was a little nervous about being a dad, but I knew Sara would be a great mom and make up for any deficiencies I had in the parenting department. Later in her pregnancy, we took a peek via an ultrasound and discovered our first child would be a boy. At least now we knew what color to paint the nursery.

Those early months of Sara's pregnancies were filled with so much joy and anticipation. This may sound crazy if you don't know me real well, but when Sara was in bed or on the couch I would lean over and put my face right in front of her belly and sing to my son, complete with a DJ's patter: "That was 'Love Me Do' by the Beatles." Life couldn't have been better for both of us. I was doing well at Southwestern, Sara was recruiting for me, and we both couldn't wait to welcome a new little Olson into our lives.

One miserably cold day in December I was with my boss, Allen Clements, in Oshkosh, Wisconsin. We had spent the day interviewing students and coaching our student sales leaders. After a nice dinner, we walked back to our hotel in a biting wind sweeping across Lake Winnebago. Exhausted, I flopped into my bed, shut off the lights, and promptly fell asleep, only to be startled awake about an hour later by the shrill ring of the phone (no smartphones where you can pick out a nice, soothing ring tone—these were real landlines with claxon-like rings). It was Sara, who had been waiting all day to talk with me.

"Honey..."

After that single word, all I heard was sobbing.

"Sara, what's wrong?"

My mind raced in a panic as I imagined all the bad things that could have happened to cause her to call me in tears. After more sobs and a word or two that I couldn't understand, she calmed down enough to continue.

"I...we...the doctor got the results from our AFP test...oh JT... it's awful...they think something's wrong...they had to do an amniocentesis. Abnormal results in one direction mean Downs Syndrome, and in the other direction means either spina bifida, hydrocephalus or anencephaly...which can range in severity from needing to shunt fluid from the brain, to an inability to walk, or death within hours of birth."

As her words tumbled out, I could almost feel my heart stop beating. I just kept repeating silently to myself; something's wrong...something's wrong. This couldn't be happening. Sara's pregnancy had been pretty routine. She was in great health. And we had such great plans for our baby boy. I couldn't wait to go on hikes with him or build dams at the farm with him by my side. Or, maybe, if I was lucky, I'd get to teach him how to golf.

I flooded her with questions. Was the problem with his brain or his spine? What exactly is wrong with it? Are they one-hundred percent sure? Is it something they can fix after he's born? I also reassured her that I loved her and tried to encourage her that we would somehow get through this, but to be honest, I didn't know how.

After the initial shock, we both collected our thoughts, and that's when Sara revealed that the specific condition her doctor mentioned was called spina bifida. I had heard of it but didn't really know much about the condition, so Sara explained what she had learned from her doctor: it's a birth defect that can result in everything from an inability to walk to problems with bladder and bowel control to learning disabilities. Then she mentioned something else her doctor told her.

"You and your husband need to decide what you want to do about this pregnancy."

Meaning, we could terminate the pregnancy and not have to deal with a child who might have a difficult time learning, spend his life in a wheelchair, or have Downs Syndrome. I heard a deep sigh on the other end of the phone, and then these words: "Can you come home?"

When the sun came up a few hours later, I met Allen in the coffee shop and told him what was going on, adding, "I think I'm going to drive home right now."

This cut against the Southwestern work ethic. Unless there's a death in the family, you plow through whatever is happening in your life. We have work to do. A mission to accomplish. I fully expected Allen to try and talk me out of leaving, but I had made up my mind. Even if it would cost me my job, I was going to rush home to be with Sara. Sadly, Allen had gone through a recent family crisis of his own, so when I informed him of my plans, he just shook his head and spoke in a soft voice.

"You know what, JT? I wish I would have made those kinds of decisions when I was a young sales manager, but I didn't. Go home! I'll handle things here."

For the next thirteen hours in my car, all I could think about was my son. He wasn't a fetus. He would not be denied a chance to live and prosper. Terminating the pregnancy was not an option. So as I drove, I pictured him sitting next to me in the car, with a wheelchair in the backseat. I saw myself helping him get dressed in the morning. I'm getting used to it. Telling myself that this is my life and I'll make the absolute best of it. I see him as a teenager, perhaps complaining that he can't do things that other teenagers can do, and I already had my pep talk ready for whenever he complains about not being able to walk.

"What are you talking about? You've got plenty of opportunities. Hear that guy on the radio? That's a DJ. You could be the best DJ in the world. You've got plenty of talents. Plenty of skills. You've got a great life ahead of you."

I told myself this is not the way JT Olson wanted it, but this is how JT Olson is going to have it because God says this is who I've given you. It was as if God was saying to me, "Put your money where your mouth is. If you're going to *say* abortion is wrong for any reason, then you better walk the talk."

God transformed my mind...

That ride home was long, but it wasn't a struggle. I was totally at peace with the prospect of a son who might spend his life in a wheelchair or worse. I don't take credit for that because I believe God transformed my mind so that I viewed my son—and all unborn children—the way He did.

I got home and rushed inside to find Sara red-eyed and lying in bed in the middle of the afternoon, which is so unlike her. So I promptly—maybe unwisely—tried to share my optimism, and let's just say it wasn't working. I jumped around all excited about our boy, and she just glared at me. I leaned over and sang to her belly: "That was 'White Christmas,' by Bing Crosby." She wasn't impressed.

"JT, we just got this horrible news and you act like you don't even care! All you can do is sing and act foolish? What do we want to do about this pregnancy? Is it even fair to bring someone into this world who may struggle to make friends, who might be teased, whose life could be very difficult?"

That's when I realized I may have gotten a little ahead of myself. And her. So I sat down and explained what had happened to me on the ride home and how God showed me that this child we were about to have was His gift to us. "Sara, what we're going to do is have this baby and be the best parents to him that we can. Maybe…just maybe…God didn't give this child to us because He thought we'd be the best parents. Maybe He gave this baby to us because He knew we needed *him*. Maybe Sara Olson needs to learn a little something about patience and maybe JT Olson needs to learn that not everyone is a Type A achiever. You're not going to do this alone. We're going to do this together. As a family."

As Sara reached for me I held her tight and close. I think that's when we both knew that the news she had just received could never dampen the love we had for our son. And that maybe we were being put to the test. The culture we lived in told us that the best thing we could do for ourselves and even the baby inside Sara's belly was to terminate the pregnancy and start over. But the God we loved reminded us that whatever the outcome of our pregnancy, He would honor our decision to choose life. It's one thing to say you're pro-life, but when faced with the prospect of caring for a seriously disabled child— one that may never speak or even recognize you—it's almost as if the enemy is taunting you. But our resolve was strong because we knew our little boy was in God's hands.

> *God didn't give this child to us because He thought we'd be the best parents. Maybe He gave this baby to us because He knew we needed him.*

I stayed with Sara for the rest of the week, then joined Allen on another campus the following Monday. Sara had a follow up appointment with her doctor and once again, called me as soon as she got home.

"JT, you're not going to believe this," her voice dancing through the phone lines.

"What is it honey?"

"The amniocentesis came back perfect! The AFP was a false negative! You're going to be the daddy of a healthy baby boy!"

Of course I was happy. Thrilled. But at the same time, I couldn't help thinking of all of those other babies whose parents were told they would have serious health problems and decided to end their pregnancies. How many of those babies were just like our son, who would later enter the world kicking and screaming and completely healthy? And how many would not have a chance to overcome whatever health issues with which they were born?

I did not fully grasp the fact that every year, approximately one million women chose to terminate their pregnancies. Or that only about one percent of those abortions were performed because the baby had serious health and development issues. The vast majority of abortions are performed because having a baby seemed difficult or impossible for the biological parents who did not want to grow a child in utero only to place it for adoption with someone else—and sometimes abortions are performed for even lesser reasons than that.

Little did I know that embracing the inherent value of every life would become a theme in our marriage.

Little did I know that embracing the inherent value of *every* life would become a theme in our marriage. We faced the same question asked a different way with each child in our family.

From the moment Jeff was born he brought us joy. The students fell in love with him and had come to nickname him Jazz. He was like our organization's mascot. We even had a level of production called "The Jazz Club," affectionately named in Jeff's honor. He was sensitive and smart as a whip to boot—something he clearly didn't get from me.

It had taken several years for us to get pregnant with Jeff, and he was so beloved that we decided to try for our second child right away. By the time Jeff turned two, Sara was so hopeful for a second child that each month she would drive to her ob-gyn's office to take the earliest pregnancy test on the market. Each month she would receive the news she didn't want to hear, and would leave the office trying to convince herself of all the reasons why it was best after all—she wanted to lose weight, we had a big trip coming up, and so on. Despite her best efforts to convince herself, each month she was enveloped in the sadness that our second child wasn't coming any quicker than our first one had. Finally, the doctor ran some tests on us both and quickly discerned that there was an insurmountable problem. The first pregnancy had been highly unusual. A second would be miraculous. The doctor asked if we had ever considered adoption. The news was excruciating, especially for Sara. Every baby shower, diaper commercial, children's program in a Sunday service would take her to a place of yearning. She tried to share in the happiness of others as they announced their pregnancies, but the truth is, she wanted another baby so much it literally hurt.

Shortly after Jeff turned two, we went to Bethany Christian Services to see what we needed to do to be considered for as adoptive parents. We looked through profiles of other people wishing to have a family through the miracle of adoption. It was overwhelming! How would we ever be noticed in that intimidating stack of picture perfect dossiers? We already had one child. Would anyone consider placing their child with us when there were so many eager families looking for even a first child? Disheartened by the number of people seeking to adopt, but determined to put ourselves out there, we put together the best letter to a biological mom that we could, hoping to get noticed.

At the end of that summer, one of the students, Rose, told me she was pregnant and planning an abortion. We found this curious because she herself had been adopted. What if her mother had chosen the same thing? Somehow, I was able to talk with her about the fact that Sara and I were hoping to adopt and asked if she would consider carrying to term and allowing us the privilege of raising her baby. She agreed to the idea and we were over the moon!

In September, Sara's sister, Michelle, had her first child, Kailee. Sara went to visit her in Wisconsin to help her settle into her new normal with a baby. While traveling there, she realized that the smells of certain foods were making her sick. She wondered… after all of this time, is it possible?! Sneaking into the bathroom at her parent's house, a pregnancy test quickly confirmed her best suspicions. She wondered what they would do about Rose's baby. Having waited and wished and hoped for another child, the thought of raising two was a double blessing. We would surely just raise them as if we'd been blessed with biological twins.

I traveled up to Wisconsin later that week to hold an awards banquet for my students. This was at the very same resort in Lake Geneva where I'd surprised my bride with her engagement ring. Little did I know she had a surprise for me. Once again, following the commotion of the weekend, we found ourselves eating in the restaurant. Sara spoke to me in grave, circumspect tones. "JT, I just found out that another woman in your organization has found herself in an unplanned pregnancy…and the father is in your organization."

"Who is it?!" I probed, feeling deeply concerned.

"Guess."

"I can't guess…give me a clue."

"Well, he's short in height but tall in stature. He's absolutely central to the organization. Probably the most key guy that you have."

"Not Don Meyer!"

"Nope. Guess again."

After great pause, Sara pulled out her pregnancy test. I was shocked. We were going to have two new little babies!

When we arrived home in Nashville later that week, we received a call from Rose. She'd found out she was pregnant with a son and thanked us for helping her to have the courage to carry that little guy to term. She hesitated…she didn't know how to tell us this, but she had decided she wanted to parent him herself as a single mom. Naturally we were disappointed but we were delighted she'd chosen to usher him into the world. God had been so gracious to us to allow us to become pregnant before we found out she was not going to place her son for adoption with us. Jeff would be a big brother, and as it turns out, it was to a sister. In May of 1992, Daley Eileen Olson was born, so named for her three grandmothers: Lora Mae (Daley) Olson, her biological grandmother, Marie Ann (Daley) Seifert, the grandmother she knew, and Eileen Mattox, Sara's mom.

Little did we know this unique and beautiful miracle would become a theme of obedience and reward, over and over as we honored and fought for the lives of wee ones that would come into this world and change it. Just a few months later, in January of 1993 we would see history repeat itself in a very dramatic way.

I also did not know that our decision for life would allow other babies to live as well. But I was about to find out.

CHAPTER 10

"You Can't Change My Mind"

At Southwestern, every year during the first week in January, we always had a big company-wide meeting. Students from all over the country would flock to Southwestern's headquarters in Nashville to get fired up about recruiting a team and learning how to manage new dealers. This one particular year, I had about fifty of my students make the trip. Needless to say, there was a lot to do and very little time to get it done. At one point, one of my students, Tim, approached me, pulling me to the side and speaking quietly.

"Deb Brigham is pregnant. But it's going to be okay. She's going to get an abortion."

Whoa!

Had this conversation happened a couple of years ago, I would have shrugged my shoulders and said something like, "Given everything that's going on in her life, she probably made the right choice." But Tim's words stabbed me like a dagger. I knew that legally Deb had every right to terminate her pregnancy, but all I could think of was a tiny infant who would never have a chance to walk or talk or be rocked to sleep. I also felt helpless. Deb was one of our top salespeople from the University of Wisconsin. It was as if this horrible thing was happening on my watch and there was nothing I could do to stop it. Tim probably thought I would be relieved that we wouldn't be losing her to a maternity leave, but selling books was the farthest thing from my mind when I met with Deb later that day. Apparently she knew that I had learned about her pregnancy and her decision to abort because with her arms crossed and a defiant glare she declared, "No matter what you say, you can't talk me out of this." And she was right. I tried my best to let her know there were options that would allow her child to live, but she just shook her head until I realized her mind was made up.

As I drove home that night, I felt like a failure. After her first summer of selling in which she did a fantastic job, Deb had decided not to sell the following summer. After a few conversations with me during the school year she decided to return to the book field, and again, she was one of our top performers. But maybe if I hadn't had those conversations, she wouldn't be in this situation. If she hadn't sold books, she wouldn't have gotten involved with the father and none of this would have happened.

I called Sara and explained what had happened and how I was unable to talk Deb out of going through with the abortion. This was a Thursday, and she had arranged with a clinic in Iowa to have the abortion the following Wednesday. I thought that maybe Sara could talk to her about keeping her baby and asked her to come downtown, where the students were meeting. Within a half hour, Sara made some childcare arrangements and was sitting with Deb, who remained steadfast in her resolve to follow through with her appointment in Iowa.

Since I wasn't there, I've asked Sara to describe what happened:

*I tried to listen to her and really understand why she was so ada-
mant about terminating her pregnancy. I learned that she didn't want
her parents to know she was pregnant. She was sort of the golden child
in her family—her two siblings had proved challenging to raise and
she didn't want to add to her parents trials. I begged her to tell her
mom. Jeff was about three by then and our daughter, Daley, was
an infant. Deb knew our kids and absolutely loved them, so I said,
"As a mom, I cannot imagine my Daley going through something
like this without telling me just because she wanted to protect me. It
would absolutely break my heart not to be there with her just because
she thought I couldn't handle the pain or shoulder the burden. Deb,
your mom would want to do the same thing for you, I feel certain of
it." Though she was willing to meet with my friend, Debbie French,
an advocate for life who had nearly had an abortion herself, Deb
wouldn't budge, telling me that nothing was going to change her
mind about the abortion.*

The more I talked, the stronger her resolve.

"I can't have this baby," she lamented. "I'll lose my job."

*I almost laughed: "Deb, my husband is your boss. I can assure you
that you won't lose your job."*

"But everyone will know."

*That was an easy one. "Then move in with us and when the baby
is born, you can put it up for adoption. No one has to know."*

*I noticed a slight shift in the tone of her voice, so I tried one more
idea, one that I hadn't really thought through or had run by JT,
though I was pretty sure he would be one-hundred percent supportive.*

*"If I pay for an ultrasound, will you at least look at a picture of
the baby inside of you?"*

She hemmed and hawed before finally answering.

*"I'll think about it, but I need to get going. I'll give it some thought
as I drive home."*

*I almost panicked because I knew what driving home meant: she
would be that much closer to the abortion clinic in Iowa. Did I really
believe she would drive all the way back to have the ultrasound?*

While I didn't give up, I thought it was all but over. I breathed a silent prayer and gave her a hug goodbye.

I have a strong faith, but who would have thought that God could use Eric Clapton to get someone's attention? On the twelve-hour drive home, she heard these words from a popular song written on the loss of a child: "Would you know my name, if you saw me in heaven?" She envisioned her own child asking her those words, and right then decided she should go ahead and carry this child to term, with the thought that she would give us the honor of raising her baby! She came back to Nashville and moved in with us. All of this seemed to be God's way of not only saving a child, but giving us another one that we wanted so badly.

We still went ahead with the ultrasound because she seemed uncomfortable and unsure, as if she might change her mind any day. I had called my ob-gyn, who is also pro-life, and explained that we had a young woman living with us who was pregnant and was considering an abortion; he readily agreed to perform the ultrasound. When we got to his office, we took our place in the waiting room and waited. And waited. And then waited some more. Apparently my doctor had been called out on an emergency, but we were reassured he would return soon. However, I noticed Deb getting fidgety and feared that she would just call the whole thing off. And not just the ultrasound, but her decision to keep the child. I had to do something to divert her from changing her mind. At about that same moment the receptionist noticed that Deb was getting really impatient, so she brought us into one of the patient rooms and offered to bring us a beverage. Deb and I made small talk for a long time…too long and she was getting restless. In an effort to pass the time and to make conversation I said, "You know that JT and I have been trying to get pregnant. I think I'm going to ask them to do a pregnancy test while we're waiting."

When I asked the nurse if I could have a pregnancy test done on myself, she asked me if I thought I was pregnant, to which I replied, "Well no, not really. You may recall that we've had some fertility issues, but on my previous two pregnancies I felt a little tinge in my abdomen. I felt that same thing earlier today and thought it might be fun to get tested."

I guess the tinge must have been indigestion because the test came back negative, a result I had experienced dozens of times before. I went back into the patient room where Deb was waiting and told her that it was negative, reassuring both of us that it was okay, and in fact probably better (oh the familiar refrain so many women who have struggled to get pregnant have oft repeated to themselves), because this way JT and I would be able to adopt her baby. Soon the nurse came to take Deb for some routine blood work. It seemed as if the entire office was working together to at least show this girl the tiny baby in her belly, and I appreciated their efforts to move the appointment forward even without the doctor in the house. I accompanied Deb to the nurse's station, but when the nurse approached with the needle, Deb immediately went white and looked like she was about to faint.

I realized she was terrified of having her blood drawn. Relying on my previous natural childbirth experience, I sought to distract her by getting right up in her face and began talking a mile a minute.

"Hey Deb, look right into my eyes. How many colors can you see in my eyeball? It's going to be okay. Did I put on too much mascara? Can you see glops anywhere?" I was rambling! Anything to distract her from the needle in her arm! "It's too bad I wasn't pregnant, because then we could have been pregnant together, but as you can see from my test right here, my results are as negative as neg..."

I stopped cold in mid-sentence. I was about to say "...as negative as negative can be," but when I actually looked at my test still sitting on the counter at the nurse's station, it was positive! Somehow in the time from when my test showed a negative to when Deb started feeling faint, the results had changed from negative too positive! Unreal! I was pregnant!

The nurses were amazed! They kept asking each other, "Is this her test?"

"I think it's her test."

"Do you know if this is her test?"

"That's where I put it!"

"Has anyone else had a test done in the last half hour?"

"I don't think so."

After much chatter and excitement, they all agreed that indeed, mine was the only other pregnancy test they'd recently done...it had to be mine!

I was elated! But now what?

My mind raced. We had already made a commitment to adopt Deb's baby. We'd given up on trying to ever have another baby... and now this. Shortly after welcoming her baby into our home, I'd be bringing another one home from the hospital. The two new babies together would make four kids, four and under. Oh well. JT loves kids! I love kids! God's got this!

What I didn't know—couldn't have known—is that as Deb sat in the doctor's office, she had been making a huge decision. She wanted to be a mom. She had decided to keep her child and was agonizing over how she would break the news to us. She was so worried that it would break our hearts to not have the child we wanted.

All of this was a big surprise to both of us, but no one can convince me that God didn't orchestrate everything, right down to a pregnancy test that mysteriously changed from negative to positive.

Pretty amazing, huh? But it didn't end there. In time, not only did Sara give birth to a bundle of sunshine and endless energy, affectionately known as "Nick at Night," but in the same season, Deb gave birth to a beautiful baby girl named Ashton Ayre. Shortly after both children were born, Sara received a card from Ashton's grandmother that to this day is the single most powerful note she's ever received. It had but two sentences:

Thank you for being there when my Deb needed you most. Thank you for saving the life of my granddaughter.

Facing the challenging future of a single mom, and watching Sara be a mother to three, Deb pressed into Jesus. You know, your life may be the only Bible someone ever reads and, in this case, I think Sara's example was very helpful to Deb. By the time Ashton was three or four, she began attending a community Bible study with Sara. As she opened her heart to Jesus, He faithfully gave her a wonderful Christian man, Tim Knight, whom she eventually married, and who raised Ashton as if she were his own.

Fast forward to Ashton's graduation party, a big celebration with family and friends from all over, including Deb's mother Elaine. She fell into Sara's arms, weeping for joy, as tears of gratitude and relief streamed down her face. Ashton was now a beautiful grown woman, with goals, dreams and aspirations of her own, and this loving grandmother was overcome by the miracle and value of her beloved grand-daughter's life. It was a powerful moment, one to be savored.

. . . your life may be the only Bible someone ever reads . . .

But there was one more component to the story...Ashton's father. Todd was another one of our best salesmen. He worked with me for five summers and by the time Deb got pregnant, he had left the business and started his career with a Fortune 500 company.

When Todd heard that we had given Deb the confidence to carry this baby to term and that it would all work out, he was a little upset with me, to say the least. Word got back to me that he was steaming mad. Although he'd been one of the most important people in our organization, I didn't care. I knew Deb had chosen the high road, and nothing else—including sales pro-duction—mattered. In fact, we lost touch after that and I hadn't heard from him for eighteen years, until I walked into that grad-uation reception for Ashton.

Now I had heard that about five years after Ashton's birth, Todd changed his thinking. We all get smarter as we age, I guess. He asked if he could be involved in Ashton's life and Deb and Tim eventually said yes. I'd say those three people walked this scenario out about as well as anyone could. Lots of mercy, grace, and sacrifice involved, but they did it.

When I looked across the room at Todd, he looked up and saw me for the first time in nearly two decades, during which time we had never spoken. He had come all the way from Wisconsin for Ashton's graduation. He started walking towards me, but I still didn't know what to expect. As he got closer and closer, it was still hard for me to tell if he was going to hug me or slug me. After a moment, he smiled and stuck out his hand and we exchanged greetings. "Good to see you, Todd!" "Good to see you, JT!"

. . . you should know that there is forgiveness enough to go around.

Then he stepped back, looked at me and got real serious, and said, "I'm so sorry for the way I acted eighteen years ago. I was such a self-centered jerk. I didn't know what I was doing and I'm so glad that you and Sara were there. Ashton has turned out to be one of the greatest joys of my life. I can't imagine my life without her. If it wasn't for you...I'm so sorry...please forgive me," he couldn't finish. I just reached out my arms and gave him a big hug. "Forgiven!" I said. I could feel his shoulders moving up and down as he wept in my arms for about thirty seconds and my mind went back to 1973, that self-centered kid who high-fived the Supreme Court decision and thought, "there, but for the grace of God go I." I felt forgiveness, Todd felt it, and if you are one of the millions who weren't as lucky as Todd and I, you should know that there is forgiveness enough to go around.

Since that time, Ashton has graduated from college, moved to Dallas and is now engaged to a wonderful godly man. Though the early years were a challenge for both she and her mom, Deb would say that one of the best decisions she ever made was her courageous decision to bring Ashton into this world.

Looking back, each of our biological children coincided with someone we had the privilege of talking to before they proceeded with a planned abortion. Max, our final biological child and bringer of much joy, was no exception. Once again we got a call from one of our student dealers. This time it was a student who had sold books with us for several summers. She knew we'd helped others in crisis pregnancies and she wondered if we would be willing to step in and talk with her sister, we'll call her Mary. Once again we offered to adopt her child. Once again we found ourselves pregnant, this time with Mattox Miles Olson, a boy who would bring us countless joys over the years. And once again a mama had fallen in love with her child and wondered how she would tell us.

When Mary came to live with us, she had not completed college, but very much wanted to. Soon after arriving, she decided she definitely wanted to parent, but she wasn't sure how she could afford to do both. At that time, we were in a community group at our church, so all of the members began to pray on her behalf.

When her son was born, he was genuinely an angel. Sara and I had a condominium we could allow them to stay in while she went to school. We also invited people to help sponsor her education. But perhaps the most miraculous thing was when a couple from church stepped up to the plate in a major way. Their two children would finally both be in school as of the fall following the arrival of Mary's son. The wife had planned to reenter the workforce in some capacity, but when she learned of Mary's need, she shelved that plan and for all of Mary's undergraduate years, this saint of a woman kept this sweet little boy while Mary went to school.

If it takes a village, Mary and her son certainly had one.

CHAPTER 11

Running on Empty

One dreary April morning, we were on our way to the airport. I say we because as usual, Sara was driving and on this occasion, Nick, who was four years old at the time, and probably my biggest fan, was in the backseat. Crying.

"What's the matter, Nick?" I asked, leaning over my seat to comfort him.

"The last time you had to leave, you said it was your last trip. (I had said that, but I'd meant last trip that month.) But now you're leaving again. I thought you weren't going to go away anymore, Daddy. I don't want you to go."

And then he cried even harder.

By now we had four kids: Jeff, Daley, Nick, and Max. I'd been working for Southwestern for about twenty years, and even though I traveled a lot I always spent a lot of time with the kids whenever I was home. To be honest, it was a great career. In fact, for me it was more of a mission. A lot of guys in my position only lasted a couple of years. The few of us with a lot of tenure stayed because we not only made pretty good money but had the opportunity to mentor young people, and that was my passion. Helping young men and women develop not just as salespersons, but as human beings.

To be honest, however, I had been thinking long and hard about where all of this was leading. I was forty-one years old at the time—did I want to be recruiting and training college students to sell books for the rest of my career, and if so, at what cost? When we were first married and it was just the two of us, you couldn't ask for a better job. Even as we started our family, it provided enough income so that Sara could stay home most of the time and care for our children. Four kids are a handful for any family, but when one parent is gone as much as I was, it wears on everyone.

I gave little Nick an extra big hug, leaned over and kissed Sara, then grabbed my bag and headed into the terminal with only one thought racing through my mind: I can't do this anymore. I was missing out on too many important events in my kids' lives; I was away from Sara far more than I wanted to be. I had seen men who put their careers ahead of their families. I wasn't there yet, but I was close. I knew what I had to do, and I knew it wouldn't be easy.

It wasn't.

As soon as I returned from that trip, I went to my boss, Fred Prevost, and told him it was time to move on. I explained that it had nothing to do with the company and that I was grateful for the opportunity to work for them as long as I had, but that my family came first. I could tell from the expression on his face that he was surprised, even shocked. You have to remember, Fred had been my boss for twenty years. He was a great friend, confidante, and mentor. This was not an easy discussion. He reminded me that I was one of the company's top sales managers and that maybe I just needed to take some time off. I held my ground and told him I would finish up my responsibilities with my current sales team, which would mean that I would walk out of the office for good in about three months.

And for the next three months they did their best to change my mind. They reminded me how much I loved working with young people. They told me that it would be a lot harder starting with a new company and that even then I might still have to travel. They reminded me of our company's generous stock option and bonus plans, rightly explaining that I might not find another company with plans like those. And it didn't help that these weren't just my colleagues—they were my friends. We'd been through a lot, and as they did their best to hold on to me, their friendship was never more apparent. In a way, I think they worried about me, just as any friend would worry about someone about to walk away from a lucrative job. But every time I wavered in my resolve to leave, I saw little Nick in the backseat crying for his daddy to stay.

Over the years, I had seen a lot of my colleagues on the management side leave, and it wasn't always pretty. As in, walking into your boss's office, telling him you're leaving, and within a week or two they weren't around. That often left a void and a lot of college kids in the lurch, wondering who's going to be their sales manager, who's going to be there for them when they have questions or run into problems. That was the last thing I wanted to do, so I took great care to make sure I left on the best of terms with everyone—my students, my colleagues, and the company's leadership. In fact, I invited the colleagues I had worked closest with over the years over to our place where Sara prepared a lovely dinner so that we could part company as friends. We had a great time sharing around the table—story after story that left us all practically falling out of our chairs in laughter.

If you ever decide to leave your job, leave it well. It might also be a good idea to have something else lined up. I handled the first part pretty well, but when I walked out of Southwestern for the last time as an employee, I had no idea what was next. Everyone thought I was crazy. I thought I was acting on faith, but as I look back, maybe everyone was right. Whenever anyone asked me why I was leaving, I told them I needed to find a job where I didn't have to travel as much so that I could be a better dad and husband, and that I was sure I could find a job like that in Nashville. They usually smiled politely, but I knew what that smile meant: "Good luck!"

Because I had poured so much of myself into Southwestern, I really wasn't prepared to go out and find another job. For example, I had never read the *Wall Street Journal, Forbes,* or *Business Week*, and therefore knew very little what was happening in the rest of the business world. And maybe because I had only worked for Southwestern, in a weird way I lacked confidence. I thought of doing what a lot of guys who left Southwestern did: become a consultant. But then I thought, "Who would ever pay to listen to what I have to say?" And yet, what I learned in all those years of selling, managing, building teams, and solving problems were great qualifications for consulting. I just didn't know it. So I started looking for work the old fashioned way. Sara and I spent a day polishing up my resume, and then I began sending them out to companies all over Nashville. Except it wasn't just any resume. I added a little creative flair.

Somewhere I found stationary that was blank on one side, but on the back had promotional words and phrases printed in barely perceptible lettering: Dependable. He's the One! Innovative. Great Work Ethic. Self-starter. In today's paperless environment, that might seem corny, but it worked. Sort of. I got a call right away from a human resources guy at a local company, and while he didn't offer me job, he gave me an idea.

"JT, I got your resume," he said over the phone. "We don't have anything for you, but I loved the paper you used for your resume. Have you ever thought of doing anything with that?"

Remember those cartoons where in the bubble over a guy's head you see a light bulb? Well, the light bulb flashed brightly in my brain. Why not start my own business making and selling creative stationary? I dipped far too deeply into the severance and bonus I received when I left Southwestern and started Sublime

Ink. Get it? Our motto was: "To boldly go where no ink has ever gone!"

It was a great idea. On paper. But I needed help, so I didn't just hire another person, but made her a partner. So not only did I burn through my savings to get the paper designed and printed, but now I was paying another person's salary even as I wasn't taking a salary for myself. Sara was not real thrilled with the idea, but that didn't stop me. I just knew it was going to take off. Something tells me I'm not the only guy in the world who has thought, "I should've listened to my wife."

In the meantime, I was still looking for a regular paycheck and signed on with some former Southwestern guys who were making a lot of money recruiting for major corporations. It looked like a perfect fit—I would open an office in Nashville and basically work the phones. No travel. Good money. Again, ignoring Sara's caution, I invited a friend to join me as a business partner. She wisely explained that a good way to ruin a friendship is to go into business together, and she wasn't too far off on that one either. Early on, he saw that I was spending a lot of time with Sublime Ink. I sensed that didn't set well with him because we had agreed to be fifty-fifty partners. At the same time, my partner at Sublime Ink noticed I was spending a lot of time with my new business. So I let her buy my share of the business for a dollar. I thought I was being a nice guy all the way around, but it probably wasn't the smartest business decision I've ever made.

Something tells me I'm not the only guy in the world who has thought, "I should've listened to my wife."

The recruiting business worked for ten years, but it was tough. Really tough, and it wasn't anyone's fault. We were completely different personalities and had almost opposing visions for how we would develop our business. But we were determined to make it work, even though it was three years before we felt we could take a salary.

On the business side, it was fun. At one time we had eleven employees. I was doing what I loved—building a business, yet not having to travel so that I could enjoy my family time. Whenever we ran into barriers, we bobbed and weaved like boxers until we found a way forward. But that boxing metaphor also applied to our relationship as owners of the business, and it took its toll on everyone. I'm not proud of this, but as we grew our business, we were also creating a toxic environment for our employees. They saw that we weren't getting along, and it affected their morale.

I needed something more than balance sheets and the bottom line.

However, outside of business we were friends. We went to the same church. We were in a Bible study together. We prayed together. Even at work, every Monday morning we met for prayer in the conference room and invited anyone in the company to join us. But when it came to making business decisions together, we just weren't on the same page.

As much as I enjoyed growing the business—especially as we began to make some money—I recognized something was missing. Something that probably kept my motor running all those years at Southwestern: I wasn't doing much to help others. It really was just a job, but I wanted—maybe needed—a mission. I needed something more than balance sheets and the bottom line. And here's where it gets interesting.

Remember all those women that Sara invited into our home during their unplanned pregnancies? Many of them pondered what it would be like to put their baby up for adoption, so we found a wonderful organization, Bethany Christian Services, who sent counselors to our home to help these young ladies work through all those decisions. Apparently they were impressed with the way we opened our home to young women and asked me if I would serve on their board. It made a lot of sense to me because it would give me an opportunity to help others, something that I really felt I should be doing.

It was about that time that we began attending Fellowship Bible Church, which started with about fifty people and was growing rapidly under the teaching of Lloyd Shadrach and Jeff Schulte. We loved their teaching and the worship, but something else caught our attention. This church seemed to have adoption in their DNA. First one of the pastors adopted an African American child, and then others began adopting. It wasn't long before you could look over the congregation on a Sunday morning and see this wonderful diversity of color and nationalities—probably a glimpse of what heaven is going to look like. I thought it was really cool that so many families in our church were adopting.

So here I was attending a church that believed we are all adopted by God, and that adoption reflects God's love for us and ought to be considered by every Christian family. And I was serving on the local board of the largest adoption agency in the United States, Bethany Christian Services (BCS). Whenever I came home from a board meeting, Sara would always ask how it went. I would excitedly tell her how BCS had placed a special needs child in a family or helped find a home for an orphan from Ethiopia, and we would celebrate together. Being involved with BCS had finally given me a way to invest in the lives of others, something that had been missing since I left Southwestern. What I didn't know at the time was how much I would soon be investing in the life of one very special person.

CHAPTER 12

Amazing Grace

I'm sure you've heard the phrase, "Me and my big mouth."

One balmy summer night I drove home from a Bethany Christian Services board meeting, walked in the door and Sara asked me how things went at the meeting.

"Oh, it went okay," I began. "Our finances are pretty good. Donations are up. We've got more families expressing interest in adoption and foster care. Oh, and we learned that a set of twins was just born and they're in the neo-natal care unit down at the hospital and we're trying to place them with a family."

Sara lit up.

"Oooo, let's go down and see 'em. Maybe we..."

I stopped her midsentence.

"Whoa Sara! We can't adopt. We've already got four kids. We're just now starting to actually make some money in this new business. I mean, it's a great idea for maybe sometime down the road, but if we adopt now, we'll have to dip into our life savings. Do you really want to do that?"

That usually ended the conversation for that month, but we had the same conversation after the next board meeting. And the next. I'd get all excited about the work we were doing at Bethany Christian Services and then make the mistake of mentioning a new baby who needed a home, and Sara would get even more excited, only to have me pull out the "life savings" card.

This went on for several months until we had one of those heart-to-hearts, which usually meant that I had to just stop and listen. We men need to do that once in a while.

"Look JT, I can be happy if all we ever have are our four kids. And I can be just as happy adopting a child who needs a home. And the kids—they're all on board. They'd love to have a new brother or sister. But what I can't handle is you getting all fired up about adoption one minute, and then refusing to consider it for yourself the next. So whenever you get on board, let us know. Until then, keep it to yourself!"

The battle was getting fierce. I was a goner. I just didn't know it yet.

As I crawled from the room, I reminded myself that my bride is beautiful, wise, and kind-hearted. But man, did she have to be so darn right all the time? She pretty much told me the score for adoption at the Olson place was 5-1, and the five were tired of hearing excuses from the one who talked such a big game.

Ouch!

It gets worse. Every night during prayer time with the kids was a reminder that I was the slacker. Because as they said their prayers, I had to hear this at the end: "And dear God, please help Daddy let us adopt."

The battle was getting fierce. I was a goner. I just didn't know it yet.

What I didn't know at the time was that it wasn't just Sara and the kids who were praying about adoption. Just before Thanksgiving, Sara had hosted a fundraising dinner for Bethany

Christian Services. Because she had coordinated the effort, she served as the emcee for this beautiful sit-down dinner that featured Steven Curtis Chapman, a nationally known Christian artist. She had seated him and his wife, Mary Beth, along with a host of other adoption advocates at the same table. Among them were our dear friends, Dan and Teri Coley, who would play an important role in our story. The Chapmans later founded Show Hope, one of the largest adoption grant organizations in the country. Since Sara was the emcee and pretty visible that night, there was a discussion about us.

It went something like, "So what's up with JT and Sara? They've been on the fringes of this adoption thing forever. How come they've never adopted?"

Now our involvement with Bethany was simply a way to put our money where our mouth was on the issue of life. To do what we could to encourage mothers towards life and to support them in that decision, wherever it led. At the time, we didn't realize that there was actually a worldwide orphan crisis and millions of children in need of finding their "forever family."

Someone said, "I don't know what the story is with JT and Sara, but let's commit to pray every day until they change their mind."

And that was that, until...

A few weeks before Christmas, our church began to promote the idea of "less under our tree and more under the world's tree." Simply put, we could make an impact as a church if we just sacrificed a few gifts and redirected those funds toward charity. Each family got a video to watch about one of our missionary partners in Sudan.

The first week of December, our whole family huddled up on our bed in our bedroom to watch the video. The first half was very light-hearted. There would be, for example, a photo of a crowd of kids, many naked, but with cartoon shorts and t-shirts drawn over their bodies. A British narrator saying, "Sewh, if you've gought an extra tay shurt, throw one in your sootcase, because as you cahn see, we need a whole lot of 'em!" It was entertaining and compelling, and our kids were moved to help.

Then came the second half.

We were warned that it was pretty realistic but we thought it would be a good idea to have our kids see that not everyone lived the way we did. That was a life changing decision. The second half of the video told of kids in Sudan whose parents had been killed because of their Christian beliefs. The part that was burned into my memory was a picture of a man holding a little boy who was pretty sick. As the video zoomed in on the little African child, the man said: "To be honest, by the time you see this video, it will be too late for this one. But it's not too late to help another child." I looked around at the kids and they were all sniffling. As the video concluded, there was silence. We all just stared at the blank screen. Silence.

. . . we thought it would be a good idea to have our kids see that not everyone lived the way we did.

Five-year-old Max broke that silence. With quivering lip, he said, "You mean those children love *Jesus*, and they're trusting him for their *food*, and there… is… no… FOOD?!"

Silence.

"You mean their mommies and daddies love *Jesus*. And *that's* why they got sold as SLAVES?!?" he asked in a disbelieving voice.

Silence.

And then he said, "Well…*we* could be their mommy and daddy."

Now part of me wanted to say, "How 'bout them Packers!" But I knew that humor might not go over with this crowd and this was a pretty good chance to talk about what we wanted to do. I'm not sure who spoke next, but the general discussion leaned towards doing something, anything to raise some money.

As a family, we weren't in a position to do a lot because we were still in the beginning stages of a new business and truth be told, our kids needed some basic stuff for Christmas. After some brainstorming, the kids decided to do a lemonade stand. On a few warm Tennessee days (gotta love Nashville) they were out there selling lemonade on the golf course that runs by our house. In the next couple weeks, they raised about $180 for their counterparts in Sudan. And that was that. Or so we thought.

Fast forward to Christmas Eve. Close to midnight. The kids were nestled all snug in their beds, and Sara asked me to go up to the attic and get the stockings that we would "hang by the chimney with care." We did it every Christmas Eve.

. . . what's wrong with using a life's savings to save a life?

The attic is really some unfinished space on the second floor of our house. When we bought the house twenty years earlier, we were going to finish it out and make a couple of bedrooms. With four kids and life, and obviously poor planning on my part, the rooms never got done. Going to the attic just reminded me how I had failed to do that. Instead of two nicely appointed rooms, all I saw was stuff.

And that's when it hit me. I thought, "We've got everything we need to raise another child. Why am I so worried about the money it would take to do that? Why not go into our life's savings? We've certainly used it for less important things." I guess some prayers were being answered.

I retrieved the stockings and started down the stairway only to run into Sara who was heading up to the attic.

"Sara," I began. "I was just up in the attic and we have so much stuff up there… books and clothes and toys and cribs and strollers and car seats."

I could see her shoulders droop. She thought I was about to say that we needed to have a garage sale or just give all that stuff away.

"So I got to thinking, what's wrong with using a life's savings to save a life? We ought to do it! Let's adopt."

Boom! I couldn't believe those words came out of my mouth, but as I look back, that was a watershed moment. God put it all in perspective for me. What's important in life and what's *really* important. The moment when you start to treasure things that won't rust, blow away, or be burned. I could see her eyes fill with happy tears as she began to speak.

"Are you serious JT?"

"Yes, I'm sure."

"Can we tell the kids?"

"Yes! Of course!"

She was practically laughing through her tears. "Maybe we could put a note in each of their stockings."

Which is exactly what she did. That may have been the best Christmas ever at the Olson house. Our kids were so excited when they opened their stockings that they almost forgot to open their presents under the tree. As far as they were concerned, they had already gotten the best present ever. God had answered their childish prayers. The little brother or sister they prayed for was really going to come home.

The day after Christmas, Sara was on it like a dog on a pork chop. She called our friends, Dan and Terri Coley, who had adopted several kids, to ask them where to begin. How exactly does one go about starting the process of adopting? Not reaching anyone, she left a message. Because Dan and Terri have eight kids, she didn't think twice about the fact that Terri didn't call her immediately back. She knew Terri would call when she had a moment.

Then she actually called the Sudanese ambassador to the United States in Washington, DC. To this day I don't know how she got through to him, but they had a powerful conversation in which he simply couldn't believe anyone in the United States wanted to adopt a child from Sudan. He wasn't real encouraging, but at the end of their conversation he said, "God bless you for your good intentions."

So that door closed, but another one opened up. China. Sara had been given the book, *Safely Home*, by Randy Alcorn. It opened our eyes to what was happening there. We learned that largely due to their one-child-per-family policy, thousands of babies are abandoned every year, and they end up living in orphanages until they age-out sometime in their teens or until someone adopts them. The ultimate "pay it forward" for me. I've always been so grateful for what was done for me and my brothers and sisters. How could it have taken me so long to come to this conclusion?

"We should to go to China," I told her.

Just as the holidays were wrapping up, Teri Coley called Sara back. She was pretty fired up, "Sara! Dan and I just pulled back into the driveway from a vacation with the kids. I can't believe you're going to adopt! Wait until Dan hears this! He is going to be so excited. We've been praying every day since the Bethany Fundraising Dinner that you would adopt!" She proceeded to replay the story of the pact at that Bethany dinner to pray for us to get it figured out. Well, after five years of me hemmin' and hawin', I'd say two months of our friends prayin' was a great approach!

Naturally we turned to Bethany Christian Services, where we learned that China had put a quota on the number of children who could be adopted from China via each agency. Unfortunately, the agency had reached their quota. They referred us to another agency but continued to help us with the required home study, which is a topic in and of itself that any adoptive family can attest to. The home study process starts with a social worker from your agency researching each spouse's entire life up until the present day. It can seem intrusive at first—right down to how you organize your sock drawer—but all joking aside, it is absolutely necessary. The goal of a home study is to make sure you will be able to handle all that adoption entails, and that the child will experience growing up in a stable family. The last thing you want is to adopt a child and then discover you aren't up to the task of parenting them. Because of the training and education that takes place during the home study process, most adoptions are a positive experience for both the child and the adoptive family.

Once we passed the home study, the next task was to fulfill all the requirements on the Chinese side, known as the dossier. After all of that was complete, the only thing left to do was to wait…

Both are living proof of the fact that life doesn't have to be perfect in order to be good.

and wait we did. It was agonizing. Like the gestation of an elephant.

Because we were adopting from China, we knew our fifth child would be a girl and had decided to name her Jerene Grace Robin Olson, and to call her Grace or Gracie. (I've always been a George Burns fan. If you're still in the dark on that one, I'm sure you've looked it up on your phone by now. If you're not reading with a phone, then you know who George Burns is and why I say that.)

We knew our daughter would have questions: Why me? Why didn't my parents keep me? Why does my story have to include sadness? Thinking ahead to that moment, we named her in honor of two women who mean a lot to us. Jerene was for my sister, the youngest of five children, a girl who lost her parents prematurely in a tragic way. Robin for our neighbor, also the youngest of five children, who lost her parents prematurely in a tragic way. Both are incredible women. Both have beautiful lives. Both love the Lord. Both are living proof of the fact that life doesn't have to be *perfect* in order to be *good*. In fact, very good! Grace because of God's grace to them, to us, and to her.

If you've ever adopted, you know this waiting period can take you through an emotional roller coaster. It's that time when people come up to you and ask all kinds of questions. Questions you wish you had answers to. "When will you get her?" or "Do you have a picture?" You learn quickly to answer with grace and sometimes a wee bit of education for the inquirer. After all, even though some questions are inappropriate, the people who ask them really do have good intentions. They just haven't thought the whole thing through yet or understand the process.

Like when people asked, "Why are you adopting from China? There are plenty of kids here in the United States that need parents." Now when someone asks that question, they usually want to debate the merits of international and domestic adoptions. The truth is, God is probably talking to them about adopting and they're resisting and they want to lash out. My answer to that question was three fold.

I don't think God is making these decisions based on political boundaries.

"I don't think God is making these decisions based on political boundaries. I think he cares for the kids in other nations as much as the kids in America."

"Most orphans in America are not in the same kind of danger as kids in other orphanages around the world."

And my favorite, "Because that's where my Gracie is." That usual laid it out pretty well. I always pray for folks with those questions. Praying that they will stop being like I was and start thinking seriously about whether or not they've been called to adopt or to just be of help to those who have been called.

We started this adoption process on December 26, 2001, the day after that epic Christmas. About fifteen months later we were all teed up and ready to go to China when a health epidemic hit several countries in Asia. It was known as the SARS epidemic. Bottom line is the US government shut down all non-essential travel to some countries and China was one of them. That was like a stomach punch.

We had grown attached to Gracie. She was the topic of many discussions around the dinner table, wondering what she was doing at certain times during the day. Since China was on the opposite side of the world, her day started when ours ended. At the night the kids would pray that she would have a good day.

It was kind of funny, but Nick and Max had this little prayer war going on. Max would pray for her and then end by saying, "and please God, help her to be cute." He was seven and concerned about the optics, I guess.

Nick, on the other hand, was bit of an antagonist. His prayer would end with, "and please God, help her to be ugly." Max would be steaming and Nick would just look over and say, "We would love you if you were ugly, Max. And we'll love Gracie if she is."

We did the best we could to enjoy the wait and get our kids ready to welcome Gracie. When you're in the midst of this kind of thing, there are lots of teaching moments that pop up.

One day while driving in the car during this time, Max sparked an interesting conversation with Sara:

"Mom, I'm a Christian, right?"

"Well Max, what do you think?"

"I think I am."

"What makes you a Christian?"

"Well, I'm nice to my friends, and I share and I obey you and dad."

"Max those are all *wonderful* things, and I'm so happy that those things are true of you…and they are! Those are things that will bring you so much joy in life. If you continue to do those things throughout your life, you are going to have a really great life! But those are not the things that make you a Christian."

"But then how do you get to be a Christian?"

"The same way Gracie will come to be an Olson. Tell me how that's going to happen."

"Well, we're going to go get her."

"Yes. That's right. Then what?"

"Then we'll adopt her!"

"Yes. That's right. That's what God does for us. He adopts us. Will Grace get to be adopted because she was laying in her crib being a better orphan than the next baby? Is she being adopted because she's smarter or better or nicer or cuter?"

"No."

"Why are we adopting her?"

"Because we love her and God told us to."

"Well that's how it is with God. We get to be a part of His family just because He loves us, not because of something we do. He says He loves us and wants us to be a part of his family and all we have to do is say, 'Yes!' Well, and, 'Thank you,' might be good too!

"Do you know the best part is? When Gracie was born, the Chinese government issued her a birth certificate with her Chinese name on it. When we adopt her, they're going to issue her a new birth certificate with her adopted name on it: 'Olson'. It's as though she will have been born again, but this time as if she'd always been an Olson. She will be as much an Olson as any one of you four kids are, one hundred percent ours. Forever! Nothing will change that. In the same way, when we accept Jesus' invitation to become a part of God's family, we are born again. one hundred percent His! Forever! God issues us a new birth certificate, just as if we'd always been a part of God's family. Only instead of signing our birth certificate with ink, He signs ours with the blood of His Son Jesus who died on the Cross for all of our sins."

It still blows me away when I think about how much God taught me about His love for us in the process of adopting our daughter.

Because we love her and God told us to.

CHAPTER 13

A Season of Miracles

The summer of 2003 held a few surprises for the Olson family.

China remained closed, and we were still waiting to be matched with our little Gracie. So life went on as usual. One of the events everyone looked forward to was going to Wisconsin to spend the Fourth of July with family.

As I mentioned before, I've always been grateful to Aunt Marie Ann and Uncle Ralph for the sacrifices they made in taking us five kids into their family. On top of all that, they had the wisdom to make the Fourth of July holiday an annual tradition. All eight kids, spouses and grandkids would converge on Marie Ann and Ralph's beautiful home on Beaver Lake in Hartland. It would involve 20-30 people hanging out for three or four days. There was waterskiing, water volleyball, Frisbee tossing, football heaving, golfing, and boat rides around the lake complete with hors d'oeuvres. The highlight for the kids was the parade in nearby Stone Bank. This July extravaganza has been going on for years and has kept all of us connected. Good parenting, in my opinion.

On this particular trip, naturally, everyone was asking about Gracie. Typical stuff. When will we know? Have we got a picture yet? They were all just as excited about a new family member as we were, almost.

On Friday, the Fourth, we were all piling into the cars, trying to get this massive bundle of chaos to the parade site early enough so we could be the target of candy missiles thrown from the marchers. As we're counting heads, the home phone rings. Aunt Marie Ann answers and it's for Sara. It's THE call. The call we've been waiting on for months. Confusion abounding. Everywhere. People in cars, some in the driveway, some down by the lake, some looking for shoes, you know the drill, and we get THE call.

Sara had given the number to our agency and our social worker who wanted to give us what little information we had, knowing we were anxious to learn at least something. It wasn't much but Sara was told our Gracie was fifteen months old and from the Xingu Province. She was born on April 29th, 2002, and her finding date was May 29, 2002. That means they found her on the steps of the Number 3 School on that day. That was it, but it was enough to make Sara's heart sink.

Two things were crossing her 'mother of five' mind. And she was keeping those two things to herself.

You see we had requested an older child because we wanted her to be closer in age to our youngest, Max, who was seven, and a strong prayer warrior for cute sisters. We also thought it would be easier to have an older child since we were in our forties. Maybe I should say, *I* was in our forties. Sara still looked like she was twenty-five. She still does.

The other issue was the birthday. It fell smack dab in the middle of the busiest time of the year and three other family birthdays. Growing up in a family of eight kids, birthdays at our home were recognized and celebrated, but not the same way Sara's family celebrated. True to her family's tradition, when we have a birthday, we celebrate! I didn't think it was a big deal because I figured whatever the situation is, we'll plow through. That's the sensitive side of me showing off.

So I am all excited, the kids are excited, but Sara not so much. I noticed her on the phone a lot and found out she was trying to call her friends from a Bible study group, just to get some moral support. She couldn't reach any of them. Keep in mind there are a lot of people around and lots of kids to watch so it's not like she and I could pull away and have a deep discussion about God's Sovereignty, Free Will, Calvinism, and the Olson's choice to adopt a little girl from China.

. . . you're about to steal one from the gates of Hell . . . and Satan doesn't like it.

In fact, she was so discouraged, the next day she called the social worker and questioned whether this was our child or not. The social worker said something to her that I will never forget, that I believe with all my being, and that I've shared with several adopting families since.

"Listen Sara. I've been in adoption circles for a long time and if there's one thing I've learned as I've watched Christian families adopt. It's that you're about to steal one from the gates of Hell…and Satan doesn't like it. He knows he can't stop it, but what he can do is to rob your peace and your joy in the process. Don't let him!"

They talked a little more and the social worker encouraged Sara to pray about this and for a sign that this was indeed the path meant for us. Sara agreed, but she kept all this to herself.

The next day towards evening, as we were wrapping up another great Fourth of July on Beaver Lake, she finally gets in touch with one of her best friends who also lives on our street, Mel Tunney. They have a nice conversation. Mel's a great encourager and I think Sara felt a little better. Then Mel asked Sara, "What time are you guys getting back tomorrow?"

Sara answered, "Oh, it's a twelve hour drive with four kids and I don't think I'll see you until Monday."

Mel mysteriously replied, "Don't ask me any questions, just be home by six p.m. ....and Sara, ...be sure to have your makeup on."

The entire drive home we speculated on what that call could have meant. As per our instructions, we stopped at the Tunney's house first and Dick and Mel came out to meet us. Not a lot was said, they just jumped in the van and we backed out the driveway and headed up the hill to our house. We got out and Dick had us all line up. I was first, Sara second, and the kids behind us. We joined hands, closed our eyes at Dick's command and walked up to our front door. As we walked in the house you could smell paint so I knew something had been done to the place. We walked through the foyer, into the kitchen and stood with our eyes closed still wondering what we were about to see.

Dick finally said, "Okay, you can open your eyes."

We were floored.

Our kitchen was filled with twenty-two friends surrounding us. All of them smiling and laughing at our gaping mouths. The kitchen had been totally refurbished and some parts remodeled.

They tore off the old wallpaper, painted the walls and the cabinets, and even bought a new hutch to replace our old one. They had torn out some cabinets, and replaced the oven range. Unbelievable! The walls were decorated with all kinds of things they had each brought from their homes. They even added a huge painting on the wall that three of the women had painted. It was custom made for the Olsons.

This was incomprehensible! An epic foot-washing! Standing in that room, surrounded by our friends, we did our best to drink it all in. While we were in Wisconsin, our friends decided to redo our kitchen and we loved it.

It also explained why Sara had such a hard time reaching her friends when she was trying to reach out and process the first news on Gracie. They were all working at our house, which back then was the black hole of cell phone reception. It all made sense.

There was one other not-so-minor issue.

The Kitchen Caper team didn't want to install the new oven range because when they removed the old one, they noticed a wire cap that was melted. So they recommended that we have an electrician install it.

The next day when the electrician came by, he was visibly disturbed by the melted wire cap and of course went ahead and fixed it. As he was packing up and Sara was paying him, she mentioned that she noticed a spark frequently when she turned the pool motor on. It was the end of the day, the poor guy was all set to go home, but he went outside to look at it. After his inspection, he called Sara outside to the pump and said, "I can't go home and leave you like this for even one more night. I've got to turn this off to work on it. Stand on these rocks and if I get stuck to the switch box, don't touch me. Use this board to knock me off."

It's funny how God can use a simple act of kindness to bless someone else even further than they may see.

"Um. Excuse me! What? Were we headed toward a serious problem?" Sara asked.

"No," he replied. "You were in a serious problem. It just hadn't become catastrophic yet."

Bottom line was that our friends meant to bless us and they surely did. But God used that blessing to prevent a fire breaking out in our home and who knows what else. It's funny how God can use a simple act of kindness to bless someone else even further than they may see.

The joy-filled effect of the Kitchen Caper had eased Sara's mind about the adoption referral, but it certainly didn't damper her personal prayers for God's confirmation that this referral was meant to be our child. We all eagerly awaited the complete referral information, especially Sara.

On Monday of that week, we received a complete referral via email (no pictures, so the prayer war between Max and Nick continued). I came home at lunch to share the information with Sara and the kids. While sipping on soup, I proceeded to read the entire sheet of paper, which included the following:

Name: Yu, Xiaoshu (pronounced you-shao-SHOE)

Date of Birth: April 29, 2002

Date Found: May 29, 2002

It went on with information about her height, weight, the specifics of where she was found by the orphanage, her developmental milestones, current state of health, food preferences and personality.

Sara was still a bit hesitant to completely accept this referral and wanted to make sure this was meant to be.

I headed out the door to return to the office. Sara kissed me goodbye with a sigh as I handed her the referral papers. Her eyes immediately fell on the one word I'd failed to read:

Name: Yu, Xiaoshu "*Grace*"

With excitement she squealed, "You didn't read that word! Look! Look what that says! They don't know we named her *Grace*! I think when the Orphanage Director found her on the steps of the Number 3 School halfway around the world in Xingu China, she named her the same name we did!" Later, we had someone who knew Chinese translate the original documents and indeed confirmed that the director had named her, "Little Grace" in Chinese. We called our social worker and asked her what that meant. She said it was true. The folks at the orphanage in China had nicknamed her Grace. The one we had been calling "Grace" since before she was ever conceived! This was indeed *our* Grace. *God's* Grace. And we were being given the privilege of raising her.

Clearly, Max had won the prayer war.

But God, the God of miracles, the one Sara shook her fist at when the SARS travel ban had been imposed, *still* had a miracle up His sleeve. Besides just testing our patience, the delay from the SARS epidemic gave us time to make arrangements to take our entire family, all four kids, to China when it reopened six months later.

Our family was in the first group of adoptive families to travel after the ban was lifted. Since the businesses in China had suffered some economic loss due to the travel ban, they were eager to entice tourists and business travelers back to China. Hotels lowered their rates to around $50 a night. One of our friends gave us almost $2,000 of airlines vouchers, and still other friends pitched in so that we could afford to go get Gracie as a family. It was one of the most unusual things I have ever experienced, but people would come up to us and give us a check and say something like, "We're not in a position to adopt but we feel compelled to do something for orphans."

Wow! It was unbelievable, but we were about to take the kids on what I would call "the trip of a lifetime" to pick up their little sister.

"Hang on, Gracie. We're coming."

CHAPTER 14

China: A Trip of a Lifetime

The trip of a lifetime began on September 9th, 2003.

After at least twenty-four hours of flying and waiting in airports, we arrived in Beijing just as the celebration of the Moon Festival began. We checked into the Marriott, which was connected to a five-story shopping mall, and preceded to get hopelessly lost. Now that's a weird feeling. Being the dad, supposedly leading, and getting everyone lost. We didn't speak the language, couldn't read the signs, but kept asking people where the Marriott was. Somehow one of the kids figured it out and got us back to home base.

We were with a group of about twenty families who were all adopting, so the next morning we all gathered together and our tour guide laid out the plans for the next three days. The Chinese government required that we go on a cultural tour and we were thankful we did because it was awesome. We saw Tiananmen Square, the Summer Palace, real pandas at the Beijing Zoo, the

Great Wall of China, shopped at the Pearl Market, and even ate Peking Duck in Peking. That's a little like being in Tupelo when it's two below. It really was a bonus and a tremendous education for our children.

But the frosting on the cake was discovering that Dick Justmann—the guy who recruited me to Southwestern thirty years earlier—was also in our group on their way to pick up *their* adopted daughter, whom they had decided to name Sarah. It was so much fun for our families to get to know one another, but deep down, we all wanted to get our girls.

Finally, the fateful morning of September 15th arrived. We flew to Nanjing, because that's where Gracie was. It was the last flight of our lives without Gracie. We all wondered if she would recognize us from our pictures, if she would be overwhelmed by the number of siblings she would have, if she would trust us, if we would smell or look funny to her with our strange scents and long American noses.

We checked into this high-rise hotel, with instructions to wait in our room until the tour guide called us. That was supposed to be at six p.m. The plan was for the orphanage to bring the babies to a conference room in the hotel where all the families would be given their new child. We waited and six p.m. passed with no call. There was a lot of pacing going on in that hotel room. Sara finally decided she wasn't going to wait anymore. We all went down to the front desk to see what was going on and all we could hear were babies crying. We looked up to the third floor balcony, where all the commotion was and saw a worker holding this cute little Asian princess. Sara recognized her right away.

"That's her!" she cried pointing to the daughter she'd never yet met, and sure enough, there she was in blue footie pajamas and pigtails, the cutest little mass of hair and pouty lips you have ever seen. Sara raced up the stairs and we all followed. We got to the room, showed our papers and Gracie was placed gently in Sara's arms, crying her eyes out. After a few moments, Sara handed her to me. In that moment, she wasn't our adoptive daughter. She was ours. Period.

As I held this crying little girl, the only thing I could think to do was sing to her. That trick had worked with all the other kids when they were little. I was overlooking the obvious though. She didn't know any of the songs and probably didn't appreciate what a great singer I was.

She kept crying and I resigned myself quickly to the fact that that wasn't going to change. I remember it like it was yesterday. I held her and then looked down at my four other kids. I slowly turned to look each one of them in the eyes. They all had huge tears running down their faces. They loved this little girl and it broke their hearts to see her so sad and scared. We had all come a long way to get her.

Somehow in God's great providence, He knew how much I needed grace . . . and Grace.

I had probably come the farthest. All those excuses for not adopting seemed so small, so insignificant. Somehow in God's great providence, He knew how much I needed grace... and Grace. How much we all do. I imagined a distraught Chinese couple who had already completed their family and then discovered another child would soon arrive. I'm so grateful that they decided to have the child anyway and left her to be found, giving her the gift of life. Every Mother's Day I think of four mothers. My mom, my Aunt Marie Ann, my wife, and Gracie's mom. What a gift she gave us. We arrived in China a family of six, and left as a family of seven.

Amazing. Grace.

From the moment Grace laid eyes on us, she decided she loved one of us and that the rest of our family would have to win her heart. Like a baby duck bonded to its mother, Grace connected herself immediately to Nick. She could not bear to have anyone else hold her, feed her, or push her stroller if Nick was around.

It was almost comical. When she was with Nick, she was completely content, but God forbid someone else would push her stroller. She would turn around and start scolding whoever was manning the helm and she wouldn't stop until Nick was pushing. And then she would look back every so often to make sure he was there.

Throughout our time in China, Grace eventually warmed up to Sara, Jeff, Daley, and Max, but kept a strong preference for Nick. I, however, was on the outs. I distinctly remember thinking that this is how I act with God sometimes. But He still hangs in there with me.

"She's got a year." I said. Joking of course, but deep down, I just wanted to hold her, give her some kisses and have the same relationship that I saw her developing with the rest of the family.

We made our way through the paper process in her province, and then down to the city of Guangzhou where the U.S. Consulate was located. Back then, that's where all the families from the United States had to go to get their paperwork completed. The White Swan Hotel was the one place every family who had adopted from China knew about. It's a luxurious place and we had a blast with all the kids, including Grace. But soon it was time to head home, and being a little homesick, we were all ready.

On September 26th, we woke up before the sun rose and proceeded to get all the kids ready, but there was a problem. Grace was running a fever. Given the recent international upheaval with SARS, no one was allowed to fly with a fever; everyone had to pass through a scanner and be declared fever free before they would be allowed to board. When we arrived at the airport, we quickly unpacked our luggage to find the medication. As we raced through the airport asking ourselves what we could do, making alternate plans if one of us had to stay back with Gracie, we turned the corner and ran right into an official with a hand fever scanner that kind of looked like a gun. He appeared out of nowhere.

Stunned, I think all six of us started silently praying at that point. Sometimes we want to tell God how big our problems are, but we should be telling our problems how big our God is. I was praying big. For protection and no fever.

The unsmiling official aimed it at each one of us in turn as we silently pleaded with God to allow us to get home with our little girl. Somehow, she passed the test. Each of us considers it nothing short of miraculous that we were able to board that plane. And that flight home was the longest of our lives. It was a fourteen-hour flight and she cried for thirteen of those hours. Yeah, we were that family with the crying child. Even though there were twenty other little babies, not one of them could measure up to Gracie.

Sometimes we want to tell God how big our problems are, but we should be telling our problems how big our God is.

As we touched down on U.S. soil, all my fears about whether an older couple like us should adopt, about whether we could give her as much attention or the same opportunities as the youngest of five, or worse, about what if something should happen to us, gave way to the thought that this girl was now a U.S. citizen and her life had just pivotally changed for the better. No matter what else happened, she would have food, shelter, clothing, education, opportunities, and most of all, she would always have a family who loved her. No matter what. There was some satisfaction in knowing her life had been irrevocably changed for the better, and thanked God for my Gracie and for my country.

Sara and I are both from the Midwest, so when we found that we would have a twenty-four hour layover in Chicago, we jumped at the chance. It was a family reunion with one new member. Sara's parents came down from Sheboygan, Aunt Marie Ann and Uncle Ralph came in from Milwaukee with several siblings and all their kids. The comforts of family, the beautiful spread of food that Aunt Marie Ann brought so we could eat without having to go into a restaurant, and a beautiful, soft, luxurious bed. Ah, the comforts of the good ol' USA.

After breakfast the following morning, we caught a noon flight for home, where many of our dearest friends were waiting. Our homecoming was something we'd lived in our dreams many times. So many people who had a hand in this adoption were there. The Kitchen Caper crowd, others who had encouraged us to adopt, and friends from church. A beautiful mob. It felt as if all of Nashville was there with banners and t-shirts, cookies and balloons. When we got home, we had a kitchen full of groceries, and... a newly decorated nursery! All gifts from the kind of crazy Jesus-loving people we call friends.

If you've ever adopted and brought a new child into your family, you know there are challenges.

Home Sweet Home?

If you've ever adopted and brought a new child into your family, you know there are challenges. Every child is different and every family's dynamic are different. So there is no one way that's going to work for everyone. However, my first suggestion to anyone in that situation is read everything you can get your hands on by the late Dr. Karyn Purvis. Go to the Empowered to Connect Conference that she developed and you'll be in a much better place to deal with what comes your way.

The mistake most adoptive parents make is we think the child will automatically be grateful for the new digs, the toys, the food, the opportunities that abound in these United States of America. Unfortunately, it doesn't always happen that way.

With Gracie, we learned quickly about Attachment Disorder. I am not going to explain it fully here, but the bottom line is that if a child doesn't grow up in an environment where there is loving care, touch, and comfort, they might have some attachment issues.

Gracie sure did. But we went into this adoption thing knowing it wasn't going to be a cakewalk and we were committed to do whatever it took. After a couple of weeks of going about our daily lives just as we did before we got her, we realized this was going to take some extra work. So Sara basically battened down the hatches and stayed at home with Gracie.

According to the post-adoption procedures, we were required to have a social worker come to the house and evaluate Gracie. After the first week, she came to the house and did all kinds of test and told us that Gracie was several months behind. She had developmental delays, but they resolved almost instantly with one-on-one care. For example, at seventeen-and-a-half months she could not roll over, crawl or walk—her environment in the orphanage had not afforded her much mobility. She learned to do all of those things within just a matter of days. When the social worker came back a month later, she was amazed. It seemed that Gracie got caught up pretty quick. It's amazing what good healthy food and extra care can accomplish.

She was such a joy to have around. She kept all the other kids both entertained and busy watching her, sometimes for fun and sometimes because it was their turn to watch her while Sara and I got other kids to their events and activities.

Daley was the true unsung hero for Gracie. Even though there was a ten-year difference between their ages, Daley graciously welcomed her new little sister into her world, including her bedroom. Through countless nights, Daley, who was eleven years old when we brought Gracie home, would get up in the middle of the night and comfort Gracie. Often times, Sara or I would go in to help, but there were nights where Daley stepped up and did it all on her own. Daley lost a lot of sleep those first few months, but she was a trooper. Needless to say, those two have been pretty tight ever since.

All this time, she was still rejecting me whenever there was another Olson around. So we thought of a clever way to pour a little Miracle-Gro on her love for me. Sara and the kids would do the difficult but necessary parts of parenting, like giving baths, administering medicine, saying "No," washing her little face after eating and so on, while I became the guy who took her to the park, fed her food, went on trips to the zoo and so on. I was the designated "fun guy." When we were alone together, I was all she had, so we got along great. When any of the other kids were present, she always wanted to be with them. Now I had learned all about perseverance when I was a college student selling books, but this was getting old. Never one to give up on people, I kept at it hoping for the best.

During this time, joking often about "giving her a year," I remember thinking on a deeper level than I had before about how very true it was that this was how I react to God, who has adopted me. I thought about how much it must grieve Him when we don't choose Him. It grieved me when she didn't choose me. Knowing her situation and her history, it didn't make me mad, just sad. "That's how it is with God," I thought. In my humanness, I resist Him, push Him away, want anything *but* the Father who loves me, who has sacrificed everything to redeem my life, who pays the ransom for me to be adopted as His son. The natural reaction of one who fails to comprehend that the love of the Father is extraordinary, sacrificial, utterly selfless, and pure. As a son, I have an inheritance that is sure. It is mine and I will live with Him forever in eternity. There is nothing on this earth that will deny me of that inheritance, but before I step into eternity, there are benefits of being His son that I can experience here on this earth – like comfort when I am hurt, or peace in the middle of a storm. All the same, I often walk away from Him, choosing to do things my own way, if only to prove I don't need Him; I can do it myself. Yet all the while, He waits patiently for me to come to my senses to choose Him, reciprocating the way He chose me, wishing to give me my heart's deepest desires, while I demand my own way, settling for far less than His best if only because I want to do it on my own.

Gracie was adopted. She is mine forever and she will receive an inheritance that is sure, simply because she is my child. In the meanwhile, I prayed that she would choose the benefits in the here and now of being adopted. As we sought the best way to love our new daughter, I learned to grow in God's character of loving her unconditionally the best way I could. By making it as easy as possible for her to choose to do the right thing, as I waited for her to choose to graft into our family and enjoy all of the benefits of loving us back.

I remember the day she chose me.

I remember the day she chose me. We were in the front yard playing and there were a couple of her siblings present as well as our next-door neighbor, Robin, her namesake. She fell and skinned her knee, started crying, got up and *came to me*. It was monumental. She chose her father to comfort her. Robin looked at me with wide eyes, the other kids realized what had happened too and they all clapped and cheered her on. It was finally happening. Our family was becoming whole again. I can still picture her arms reaching out to me and the absolute joy I felt as I picked her up. She chose me and I was elated. I got just a hint of what God must feel when we choose Him.

CHAPTER 15

You're Just Playing Golf

As board members of Bethany Christian Services, we all did things that were in our areas of gifting. Since I was the one whose eyes would glaze over whenever we brought the spreadsheets out, it was obvious that my gifting was in fundraising, not fund tracking.

So one year we decided to do a golf outing. There was this organization called Golf for Goodness Sake. They would help you organize the whole thing, but this one was a little different. Instead of players paying an entrance fee, they were all asked to send letters out to their contacts asking folks to sponsor them. Kind of like you see runners do when they are doing a 5K race. The players have fun and they raise money for a great cause. People who donate feel good too because they help the organization save babies.

I mailed out about 70 fundraising letters to my friends and acquaintances. One of the guys I mailed a letter to was Bill Iverson.

Bill and I were in a Bible study together. Bill is a great guy, and considering the cause, I fully expected to receive a donation. So when I saw his name on the return envelope, I eagerly opened it.

No check.

Instead, Bill had taken a marker and wrote across the middle of my letter, "JT, if you told me you were working on a widow's house, I might sponsor you. But you're just golfing. Nice cause, but not for my money."

Ouch! I've sold books door-to-door for six summers, so I understand the difference between refusal and rejection. Refusal is business. Rejection is personal. This seemed like rejection, and it stung.

Nice cause, but not for my money.

What I've always loved about Bill is that if he sees something that doesn't square with his understanding of Scripture, he tells you. I didn't realize it at the time, but Bill's response was heavily influenced by what the apostle James refers to as pure religion: "to look after orphans and widows in their distress." (James 1:27 NIV) He wasn't saying we were doing anything wrong by raising money through a golf outing. It just wasn't for him. If he was going to give, it would be to help the cause of the widows and orphans among us.

Maybe it hurt a little because in the back of my mind, I was kind of thinking, "Here I am playing golf and asking friends to send me money for a good cause; on the one hand it sounded good but on the other how did my playing golf connect with the good cause?" But then there was the idea that the golf was justified because of the cause. At the end of the day, babies who might otherwise have been aborted were being given the gift of life in a loving, caring family.

In any case, based on his response to me, we had different perspectives. Generally speaking, I've never been able to just let a conflict simmer. It goes back to that last day I saw my dad alive. We had some words, and I left without making it right, something I will always regret. Maybe I'm overcompensating for that, but to this day, I will do whatever I can to resolve a conflict. It drives Sara nuts sometimes because we'll be heading into a restaurant to have dinner with a group of friends, and if we've even had the slightest disagreement on the way, I'll stop right there and ask, "Are we okay? Can we fix this before we go in?"

So I called Bill and we talked about it, laughed about it, but he still didn't give me any money. So we were good, but the words he wrote never left me. It's like they almost haunted me. For three years those words kept going through my mind. Whenever I saw a golf tournament or 5K race or fundraiser of any kind, I always asked myself, "If they were working on a widow's house, would that be more effective? More compelling?"

I even met with different people to talk about what it would look like. I just couldn't put it all together. What could you raise money for by working on a widow's house? Something was missing.

In the fall of 2006, I ran into one of my good friends at church, Don Meyer. Don was one of my top sales guys from Wisconsin when I was with Southwestern. We always made a great team. I was the visionary leader; he was the detail guy who always followed through and got things done. He eventually moved to Nashville for his work, even attending the same church as I did. I hadn't seen him in a couple of months, so when I bumped into him at church, I was eager to get caught up. Like they say, timing is everything.

"What's up, Don?"

"We're adopting four kids from Moldova," he said. Don explained that he had just returned from a mission trip to Moldova. They served with a non-profit called Sweet Sleep, which provides beds to orphans. While he was there, he grew pretty close to a little eleven-year old boy, Gheorghe. Don called his wife, Mary, who was also one of my students from the book business, and they decided to start the adoption process. In the process, they learned the boy had three siblings. Don told me, "We knew we couldn't separate Gheorghe from his siblings, so we're going to adopt all four of them."

Of course, that was music to my ears. I'm the last guy on earth who is going to say something like, "Are you sure about this?" As an orphan from a large family, I have been forever grateful to my aunt and uncle for keeping all five of us kids together, so what Don was doing really got my attention. My immediate thought was here's a guy who is really trusting God.

Sixty-five thousand dollars by the time we're done . . .

"That's great, Don!" I exclaimed. "Do you know how much it's going to cost?"

"Sixty-five thousand dollars by the time we're done," he answered.

"Do you have any idea how you're going to pay for that?"

He shrugged his shoulders and looked me straight in the eye and said, "I have no idea."

"Well I think I've got an idea," I told him.

All of a sudden it hit me! This is it! The struggle with Bill's words to me lifted. Instead of asking people to send me money to play golf, why not fix up a widow's house? I had absolutely no idea how this would work, or even if I could find a widow. But I was determined to somehow help a widow while we helped Don adopt four orphans.

The next Saturday, Don and I sat down for a couple of hours and discussed the whole process. How we would do it, where would the funds go, etc. As usual when working with Don, all the loose ends seemed to come together and we had a plan.

But there was still one more loose end to tie up. What will we call it? And then out of nowhere, God turned on a light bulb in my brain. Both Hands! I'll call it "Both Hands." We're helping a widow and we're helping an orphan. I can't say that I put the name through some focus group or surveyed anybody. I just *knew* that Both Hands was the perfect name. Then shortly thereafter, I came up with our motto: One for the widow, one for the orphan.

I guess that marketing degree all those years ago was paying off. But, honestly, I know God gave me the name and the motto because it so perfectly tells our story.

I began asking around, and a friend referred me to a charitable organization that provides food for hungry families. I followed up with them, and they gave me the name of a woman, Ms. Lucille, whose husband had died and was living in an older house in Franklin, a quaint little town just south of Nashville. He gave me her phone number, so I called her and arranged to meet with her.

When I walked into the house it was obvious to me that we could help her. We might not be able to do everything that needed to be done, but we could do enough to make a difference. I told her about our plan, the kids from Moldova, and how much it costs to adopt. She was so sweet and grateful that she would be considered for the project. I told her to think about it and call me and let me know if she would like us to help.

Several weeks went by with no response. And then I got a phone call from her daughter who agreed to meet with me at her mother's house. So I called Don and another friend, and we went to Ms. Lucille's house.

When we got to the house, two things became crystal clear to me. We could definitely make an impact on this house. The front porch needed to be painted. The chimney was in dangerously rough shape. There was a dead tree in the backyard that needed to be taken down. The kitchen faucet leaked. The floors were sagging so much some of the doors wouldn't close. And then there were the heaters. Five individual kerosene heaters throughout the house. A looming fire hazard. They would need to be replaced with a single unit.

The second thing that became clear to me was that this widow's daughter did not trust us. And who could blame her. Older persons—especially widows—are sitting targets to so many scammers and con artists looking to make an easy buck. As far as her daughter was concerned, I was just another shady guy trying to separate her mother from her money.

After an icy greeting, we walked through the house to make a list of all that needed to be fixed before I sat across from them to answer any questions they might have. The daughter had a master's degree from Vanderbilt University, and did her best to intimidate me by grilling me about my intentions.

"How much is it going to cost us?" the daughter asked.

"It won't cost you or your mother anything," I answered. (I always love saying that part.)

"Sounds too good to be true—what's the catch?"

"There is no catch," I explained.

Momma, it's just a blessing!

"Where are you going to get all the supplies from?" she persisted.

"We're going to ask local businesses to donate them."

"And you're really going to replace these old heaters?"

This felt more like an interrogation than a meeting to determine how I could help her mother.

"Yes ma'am."

"And fix the porch?"

"Yes ma'am."

"And tidy up the back yard?"

"Absolutely, ma'am. We want your mom to be safe, comfortable, and happy."

She sat stone-faced for almost a minute before turning to her mother and announcing, "Momma, it's just a blessing!"

The ice had thawed and she finally saw the light. Her mom was part of the team. Without her, we couldn't do this, and we were just looking for someone to serve. So now we had our widow. Next up was to organize a team of workers, and I turned to a reliable source. Don and I recruited a bunch of old Southwestern guys who lived in Nashville. I explained that they would have to send out letters asking for donations to help Don and Mary adopt four orphans from Moldova. And then show up at the widow's house to begin the makeover.

But before we could start working on her house, we needed supplies. I sent a message to the team and then they all started getting back to me about all the things they could bring. Some of them contacted local businesses and they gave enthusiastically. One of the guys even found a tree service that would send a crew over to take down that tree in the backyard. By the time the appointed Saturday rolled around, we were ready.

We started at eight o'clock in the morning, and by six o'clock that evening, we were done. For me, one of the operational highlights was removing the tree from the top down. It took them all of an hour and normally would have cost about a thousand dollars. They did it for free. We took out all the kerosene heaters, cut a hole in the wall, and installed a modern heater like you find in a hotel room.

Earlier I had arranged for the widow and her daughter to have lunch at a nice restaurant that donated the whole thing. We had someone get a manicure gift certificate so she and her daughter were able to do that. On top of all that, I had a friend who owned a limo service and he donated the use of a limo for the day. I'll never forget the look on both their faces when the limo pulled up to take them to lunch. Ms. Lucille was so surprised and grinning from ear to ear. When they came back, about three hours later, our exhausted crew was there to watch them as they got out of the limo and stared at the house in disbelief. I walked Ms. Lucille through her whole house and she couldn't believe all that had been done. She was so grateful and downright giddy. Everyone was laughing and giving each other high-fives.

When I say everyone, I probably need to explain. As I learned when we adopted Gracie, once you're approved, you can get the call at any moment: your child is ready. And when you get that call, you have to hop on a plane and go, ready or not. About two weeks before we had planned to restore the widow's house, Don and Mary got the call. Off they went to Moldova, returning about a week later. How cool was it that at the unveiling of the widow's refurbished house, Don, Mary and their four new children, along with their three biological kids, joined in the celebration. The kids who were adopted were actually there helping!

Pure religion: the widow and the orphans. And a handful of ordinary people with blisters and big smiles. It really doesn't get any better than this, except it does.

Those letters our volunteers sent out asking for donations to help Don and Mary adopt? The total cost of the adoptions came in around $90,000. I had hoped to raise about $20,000, but I guess my faith was off a little. We raised over $55,000, and after the video was sent out so everyone could see what we did, more money came in until we eventually raised about $74,000! In retrospect, I think God was trying to get my attention. As if He was saying, "JT, widows and orphans… ring any bells?"

Pure religion: the widow and the orphans.

Naturally I was thrilled to see what God had done. I really had no idea what I was doing. I guess you could say I was just trying to resolve the conflict that Bill Iverson's words had aroused in my soul; working on a widow's house. Bringing joy to someone else in need instead of focusing on something that brought just me joy. This time, we weren't just playing golf. We really did help a widow. And on top of it, we helped provide a loving home for four orphans.

And about Bill. I sent him a letter and told him we were working on a widow's house…and yes, he sent us a check.

As I headed home that evening, I decided that I would probably never do another golf fundraiser. Nothing against them. They are great fun and raise money for many worthy causes. Just not for me. My annual charity event would follow this same model—get a crew to fix up a widow's house and have them recruit donors for an orphan. I asked God to help me find another widow and to send someone who needed help with an adoption and learned an important biblical truth: Ask and you will receive – a.k.a. be careful what you ask for.

CHAPTER 16

Jumping Off the Cliff

If helping widows and orphans was energizing, going back to work was just the opposite. Don't get me wrong. Our recruiting business continued to thrive, but the gulf between my partner and I continued to grow. To this day I don't know how to explain how two friends who love the Lord and worship together in the same church have difficulty seeing eye-to-eye in the marketplace, though I suppose it shouldn't surprise anyone. Remember Paul and Barnabas in the New Testament? What began as a wonderful friendship turned into a sharp disagreement resulting in them both going their own ways. We don't know all the details of their disagreement, other than it wasn't theological. Both loved the Lord and were committed to the gospel, but found themselves on opposite sides of a judgment call. I guess if Paul and Barnabas—two of the earliest missionaries of the church—couldn't resolve a personal dispute, we were in pretty good company. With each passing day it became apparent that on some really important matters, we would never agree. One of us would have to leave, but I guess to our credit, we stubbornly forged ahead.

It was around this time that a couple of good friends from church, Greg Murtha and Dick Gygi, offered me the gift of some straight talk and expert advice.

"JT," Greg said. "You're in halftime."

"Oh yeah?" I responded. "What's that?"

Instead of telling me, he and Dick arranged for me to attend an event in Memphis where I met some folks from the Halftime Institute, an organization started by Bob Buford, the author of the book, *Halftime*. This Dallas businessman had begun a movement of men and women who have reached a level of success and yet find that it hasn't delivered what they thought it would. It was at this event that I heard a speaker by the name of Bob Muzikowski say something that hit me hard: "It's hotel earth here," he said. "We're not going to be here forever, so we need to make an impact now."

I also met successful people who had quit their jobs or sold their businesses so that they could invest their time, talent, and treasure into things that really made a difference in the world. I wasn't real sure about the talent and treasure thing, but I had a sneaking suspicion that I might eventually have some extra time on my hands. As in unemployment. But the more I listened to these people share their stories, the more it made sense to me. I had enjoyed a successful career at Southwestern where maybe the greatest reward for me was being able to offer guidance and motivation to young people. And despite the relational issues at the recruiting business, I had experienced a lot of success. But just as Bob Buford discovered in running his family's highly successful cable television business, success isn't all it's cracked up to be.

Greg and Dick were right—I *was* in halftime; somewhere between success and significance. My soul was yearning for something more than money.

An encouraging thing for me was all the men and women at that meeting who affirmed the Both Hands concept. Fortunately, we had put together a video from the first project and I got to show it to everyone. They loved it! So it wasn't just me who thought this unique idea might have some wings.

Sara and I drove home fired up about what might become of this Both Hands thing, but honestly quite frightened because there were a whole lot of obstacles. God was obviously working on my heart, but the husband/father/provider side of me was saying, "Whoa! We've got five kids at home and one of them is in college with others headed there soon. Is this the right time to do something like this?" Then my heart would say, "Where's your faith, man!" It's like there was this classic angel/demon conflict going on right there, on my shoulders, just like it's always depicted in cartoons. All I wanted was a sign or something that this wasn't just crazy thinking. That it could be possible to provide for a family and make an impact on the lives of orphans and widows. To start yet another company, but this one was going to be a non-profit. Sara and I prayed for guidance, answers, and provision.

That November of 2007, I decided to go ahead and form a non-profit, even if I wasn't sure what it would do. So I sat down and tried to draw up some bylaws and organize my charity, mostly by doing some research on the Internet. One thing I learned about the Internet is that it can give you just enough information to make you think you know what you're doing. But we got it started.

Around Christmas of that year, I got a call from a friend who Sara and I had been close to. She and her husband and their family had gone through several trials, and we did our best to help them at the time. After we talked for a bit on the phone, she said she had a Christmas card for us but wanted to deliver it in person. Could we meet somewhere? As you know, holidays are hectic, and we did our best to find a time to meet, to no avail. We finally agreed to meet at the parking lot of the YMCA about halfway between our houses.

I climbed into her SUV and we talked a little bit about our families and such. Then she handed me our Christmas card and said, "Open it, JT."

As I did, I understood why she wanted to deliver the card in person. My chin hit the floor as I saw a check made out to Both Hands for $50,000.

"We believe this is something God wants you to do, so use it for whatever you need," she smiled.

Of course I was ecstatic, and thanked her profusely. But as I climbed back into my car, I was almost overcome with fear. I had asked God to show me a sign, and you couldn't get a clearer signal than this. I felt like there was this huge neon billboard over my head. Which meant one thing: there could be no turning back. And that was more than a little scary.

We believe this is something God wants you to do, so use it for whatever you need.

Shortly after returning home, I got a call from Bill and Lisa Kersey, some friends from Southwestern. Bill actually designed our official Both Hands logo and first website. They heard about the Meyer's project and asked if I would help them do a project for their family. They were adopting from Honduras. They selected the widow, someone we all knew very well: Diana Beach. Diana's husband was my son's English teacher. He had recently lost his life in a car accident, leaving her with two kids and a house that needed a lot of work. We put the call out and this time fifty-two people volunteered!

I'll never forget that Saturday in April. I know it was April because it was the date for Daley's Junior Prom. Late in the afternoon, I slipped away from the project to observe the picture-taking rituals. I did my fatherly duties and rushed back just as the project was finishing up. The crew did a fabulous job sprucing the place up and hauling away a lot of stuff that Diana no longer needed or wanted. We painted, upgraded, fixed nagging little problems, but the biggest job was putting on a new roof.

Just as the sun was beginning to slip beneath the horizon, I climbed up on the roof to admire the work of our experienced volunteer roofing crew but my eyes caught something else. There, lining the street in the fading light were nineteen cars. I know, because I counted them. And because the sight of that many cars recalled an image I had seen nearly forty years earlier as I got off the school bus at the family farm, one that I will never forget: nearly a dozen tractors crisscrossing the fields, driven by neighbors who wanted to make sure the Olson boys got their crops in despite the fact that they were orphans. It all came back to me in that moment on the roof.

It all came back to me in that moment on the roof.

Full circle.

That night, Sara and I went out for dinner, and I was like a schoolboy who had just got back from attending his first big-league baseball game where he caught a home-run ball from his favorite player. I couldn't quit talking, I was so excited. And I wasn't just recapping the day's successful project that benefitted a widow and would provide money for a couple to adopt another orphan. For the first time, I began to lay out how I thought this was the something that was missing in my life. That maybe I could do this on a regular basis so that we could help more orphans and more widows. That I thought God was giving me this vision for how I could lead such a ministry. Sara listened patiently, even sharing my excitement, and then at one point interrupted me.

"JT, you are positively aglow."

I've never had anyone comment on my glow, but she was probably right. I was really pumped about this idea of leading an effort that would benefit two things so close to my heart. Encouraged by her observation, I continued to dream out loud.

I explained how our church was so tuned in to adoption that we would have a readily available source of couples who needed help funding their adoptions. And already I had been learning about other widows who seriously needed a crew to come in and fix up their homes. This would be the perfect time for me to quit a job that was sucking the life out of me and start a non-profit organization dedicated to helping orphans and widows. It all made sense...to me.

"Um, honey," Sara began after I calmed down a bit. "What about health insurance for our family? And that little thing we call a paycheck—have you thought about that? I know we have that big donation to start it, but with five kids what happens after that is gone?"

Of course, she was right. She usually is. She loved my idea and was totally supportive, but this was a scary thing for us to consider financially. And I remembered something that was emphasized at the Halftime event: make sure your spouse is in on your big plans. Frankly, I needed her wise words of caution because I hadn't given much thought to how I was going to pull this thing off. I had never led a non-profit before. Would I need to find office space? Hire people? And if so, how would I cover the cost of all that? All I knew was that somehow I was going to pour myself into a ministry that would help widows and orphans, and it turned out that Sara was fully on board too because as we left the restaurant, she grabbed my hand and squeezed it.

"I feel like I just got my husband back."

I knew what she meant. For the past ten years, I had let my job with the recruiting business get the best of me. I often came home with all the baggage from work and dumped it on my family—not literally, but I wasn't always the nicest guy to be around at home, and I really regret that. Remember, I'm the guy who used to fire up my sales teams by telling them, "You may not be able to control things around you, but you can control your attitude." And for most of the time I did—I'm usually a pretty positive guy. But I regret the times I let my job get to me and then spilled my frustrations onto my family. Fortunately, Sara cultivated a lot of grace in our family during those years, and patiently waited for the real JT to show up. To be honest, I was pretty glad to see the real me reappear. I had no idea how I would turn this dream into a reality, but it sure grabbed ahold of my heart and wouldn't let go. I'm not one to talk a lot about God speaking to me, but I genuinely felt He was telling me, "It's time. Just trust Me."

With the money we had been given, I found a lawyer who was skilled in opening up non-profits. I showed him my efforts to file and he promptly thrust them aside and said, "We need to do this right."

I had always wanted to name this effort Both Hands, the idea being one hand for the widow and one hand for the orphan. My attorney made sure Both Hands met all the requirements for a non-profit, giving it the formal name of Both Hands Foundation. I sort of wish he wouldn't have added "foundation" to our name, because when people think of a foundation, they think boatloads of money. But even if we missed that boat, it was comforting to know that we were legal. But I was still hesitant and having trouble pulling the trigger on leaving the business.

Next, I convinced some friends to join my board, and everything began to fall in place. Even though Gracie was just starting kindergarten, Sara decided to return to the work force and took a position at Belmont University. Max was in seventh grade, but we were homeschooling him, so in addition to getting Both Hands off the ground, I would walk Gracie to and from her bus stop every day, and help Max with his schooling. Fortunately, he was a good student and didn't need much help. The plan was for me to work out of a home office, but another friend and board member, Ty Osman, stepped forward and offered me some free office space whenever I needed it. The pieces were all falling into place, but I was still hesitant.

In the spring, I was sitting with my Bible next to the fire pit in the back yard. Some people have a prayer closet. I have a prayer fire pit. Ty walked past carrying a forty-pound backpack as he was training for a big elk hunt. He stopped, sat down, and for the next ninety minutes we talked about Both Hands, the recruiting business, and the future. He knew I was hesitant, unsure, so he asked me directly, "What's stopping you?"

I admitted that I was afraid it might not work out, and his response woke something up in me.

"Okay, so now we know the problem. You're afraid."

Okay, so now we know the problem. You're afraid.

Boom!!! And that's when it hit me. For twenty years I counseled college students about facing their fears, and it was like a voice speaking to me: "JT, it's time to face your fears. You talk about having faith. Now it's time to exercise that faith."

Have you ever watched those mega-high-dive contests on television where guys climb up a tower to a tiny platform that appears to be about a gazillion feet above a landing zone into a pool of water that seems to be about as big as a quarter? Despite all the support I had and the assurance that God would provide for all our needs, I felt like that guy standing on the edge of that diving platform. Except I was holding onto the tower for dear life, scared to death. What was I afraid of? Failure. It's what most of us are afraid of and what keeps most of us from doing things we know we should be doing. We should be thinking, "So what if I fail? It's not the end of the world. Everybody who has ever done anything worthwhile has failed. Failure is an integral part of success."

Not pursuing a goal because we are afraid of failure is like planning a vacation and sitting in your driveway, waiting for all the lights to turn green. That sounds like a ridiculous plan, but that's what sometimes happens to great ideas. When we plan a trip, we establish the destination and plan the route. If we come to a red light, we stop until it's green and then move on. But in the real world, the fallen world, we're afraid of obstacles, opposition, and what people might think.

I was afraid.

Then I remembered the joy in the eyes of the widows we'd already helped. The picture of those kids from Moldova being brought into their forever family. For me, that's some pretty powerful motivation and that's where I decided to keep my focus.

All that stood between me and the formal launch of Both Hands was my current job. As undesirable as it was, it represented a comfortable income. It's one thing to have a dream, but when following it means severing ties with a company you founded and help to build, it makes you stop and think. In a way, I wish we could have found a way to move past our differences, but maybe in God's providence and timing, the best solution for everyone—including countless widows and orphans—would be for me to leave. It wasn't easy, but toward the end of the summer, my partner and I amicably parted ways.

I released my grip on all that holds us back from experiencing the best God has for us...and jumped.

On August 18, 2008, Both Hands officially began with one unpaid employee: me.

Not pursuing a goal because we are afraid of failure is like planning a vacation and sitting in your driveway, waiting for all the lights to turn green.

In fact, I didn't take a salary for the rest of that year, but God was good on His word. We never went hungry or missed a mortgage payment. I never missed a bus run with Gracie. Max cruised through our homeschool seventh grade. Best of all, we conducted four projects that fall. Four widows experienced the love of God through a lot of elbow grease. More orphans found themselves in loving, caring families. And a whole bunch of people—including me—were having the time of our lives.

Mark Twain once said, "The two most important days in a person's life are the day they were born and the day they find out why." When I jumped off that cliff, I found out why I was born. It's almost like God was telling me, "This is what it's all been about. You have been prepared for this. Being an orphan, being taken into another family, your careers that have honed your skills at working with people, Gracie's adoption, the time is right now...jump!

CHAPTER 17

God Must Really Love Me

Over the years since we started Both Hands, we've done hundreds of projects in over 40 states. It's amazing to see what happens on each one. From my perspective, based on what families tell me, it seems there is at least one miracle on every project. Something about working on a widow's house to bring an orphan into a forever family seems to bring out the best in people.

I remember during one project in Chattanooga that the widow accepted Christ. I didn't see that coming and my eyes tear up every time I think about that one. I'd love to tell you all the stories from these projects and who knows, maybe there will be another book devoted to that topic someday. For now, I want to share just a couple of stories to give you a feel for what happens when people step out in faith on the journey of adoption.

Anthony and Hannah Opliger had talked about adoption almost from the day they were married. Anthony pastors a church in Ft. Wayne, Indiana—his wife, a registered nurse, currently has chosen to stay home to care for their daughter, Shalom.

"We talked about it," Anthony recounts. "But it was really more of an idea than a concrete plan."

Soon after they were married, Shalom entered their lives, and the plan was to bring another child into their family. Except that plan wasn't working so well.

"After about a year of trying, it became clear that if we really wanted another child, it would have to be through adoption," Anthony explained. "But still, we really didn't do much about it until we heard a man who had incurable cancer speak about adoption, encouraging all of us to open our homes to children who need a forever family. That really motivated us to begin taking steps to adopt." It seems that every story has a watershed moment when a light goes on and a mom and dad decide—it's time!

Like most couples who begin to look into international adoption, they were surprised at the cost—often between $20,000 to $40,000 or more. Pretty steep for a pastor's salary in a single-income family. They soon discovered, however, a couple from their church who had found a way to raise funds for their adoption (I love it when that happens).

"We visited with them and they told us about this organization called Both Hands and how it helped them put together a project that not only raised the necessary funding for their adoption, but also provided a much needed service to a widow. Being a pastor, I knew all about pure religion, as described in James 1:27. We signed up right away, and also decided to adopt from the same country as these friends from church: the Democratic Republic of Congo."

The Opligers contacted NeighborLink, an organization in their city that connects people in need with those who can meet those needs. That's where they met Sharon, a wonderful woman who'd experienced more than her share of tragedy. First, her son had been murdered in their garage, and Sharon couldn't bring herself to go into that garage ever since. Then within a year of her son's death, her husband passed away after fighting cancer. Among other things affected by these tragedies, Sharon's house and property were in serious disrepair, giving the Opligers plenty of work to do, requiring lots of volunteers.

"When I put the word out that we needed volunteers to help fix up Sharon's place, the response was overwhelming," Anthony told me. "To be honest, the hardest thing for me to do was to ask them to contact their friends and ask for money to support our adoption. But they never hesitated—each volunteer sent out dozens of letters asking their family and friends to donate." It never ceases to amaze me, but people get it. That we're not all called to adopt, but we are all called to care for widows and orphans.

Anthony and Hannah spent some time at Sharon's place before the project to identify the kinds of things they would need to do to fix it up.

"I was actually afraid to go into the garage," he recalls. "No one had been in there for three years—it was a total mess. And the house needed a lot done—painting, plumbing, landscaping; I wasn't sure we'd be able to do everything in one day."

On the appointed date for the project, however, everyone who signed up showed up, and more. Parents brought their kids—some as young as six or seven years old, and they even pitched in. A local refuse company gave them a big discount on a dumpster which was filled to overflowing by the end of the day. A church member who owned a landscaping business led the effort to not just clean up the yard, but also plant flowers and shrubs to make it stand out in the neighborhood.

About halfway through the day, the garage had been completely gutted and cleaned up. Anthony knew how Sharon had avoided going near it, so he stopped everything and called all the volunteers into the garage. Then he gently escorted Sharon into the structure that previously had been only a reminder of her loss. And here's where the Opliger's story takes a special twist.

"Sharon and her family once attended North Highland Christian Church, pastored by Bob Yawberg," Anthony explained. "When that church planted Broadway Christian Church, Bob became their pastor. That church, in turn, planted Northeast Christian Church, and that's the church I pastor."

Anthony had contacted Pastor Yawberg, inviting him to come and pray at a special service in the garage—sort of a dedication and turning point for Sharon, redeeming what once was only a symbol of pain for her.

"It was really a moving moment, coming full circle in the life of a widow who had been through so much."

By the end of the day, the house, garage, and yard looked almost new. When Sharon saw it, she couldn't believe the improvements the team had made in such a short time. But perhaps the best "result" of the day's hard work came in her comment to the team: "I guess this means God really loves me."

Gets me every time.

That's a big win for the widow. How about the orphan? To the Opliger's almost disbelief, more than $25,000 was raised to help them pay for their adoption.

"We thought that maybe about 100 people would donate, but more than 500 sent us money, many who we didn't even know."

The rest of the story is not as rosy.

"Technically, our adoption was completed long before we could bring Sagesse home," Anthony explained. "Sagesse—French for wisdom—remained in the Congo. We visited him twice, but the government had yet to sign his exit letter, and without that signed letter he cannot legally leave the country. On our last visit we had to quickly find someone to care for him because his foster family left unexpectedly. Fortunately, we found a godly woman to take care of him until he is able to leave."

When Anthony shared this with me in early 2015, he was optimistic that the letter would be signed soon, but he also acknowledged that this part of the experience has been difficult.

"My faith in the Lord has been stretched, but that has actually been a good thing. The Lord has shown us in so many different ways that he's with us in the midst of it, and one of the big ways he's done that is through the people in our church who have come alongside us. We feel much loved. The Lord is with us and so we continued to trust that Sagesse would join us soon."

In the meantime, as they waited for Sagesse and continued to trust, God surprised them with a little gift, perhaps to remind them that he's got their family in his capable hands. Hannah became pregnant and gave Shalom another brother: Moses.

Isn't that just the way God works?

Update

As in most adoptions, there are always obstacles to overcome. I wanted you to see that part of the journey so you would appreciate this next part.

On December 21, 2015, two lawyers from the Congo accompanied Sagesse on a flight to Washington, DC, and then on to Chicago. Despite the fact that the government had refused to grant exit letters to the hundreds of other adoptees waiting in the Congo, Anthony and Hannah received word that Sagesse was given the highly coveted—and legitimate—exit letter, which allowed him to finally join his new family.

"In the truest sense of the word, it was *unbelievable* after all that time to drive to Chicago's O'Hare International Airport and see our son," Anthony exclaimed. "We had been to the Congo twice, always having to leave him behind. But now we were able to take him back to our home where my family and a lot of friends welcomed him."

Initially, Anthony reports, those early days were challenging. Imagine being in an unfamiliar place where no one speaks your language and almost everyone you see looks completely different than what you are used to. At four years old, by all counts, however, little Sagesse is doing remarkably well, learning English, attending preschool, and enjoying getting to know his new siblings.

"Toward the end of his first week with us, I looked over at him and said in French, the language he understood, 'You are my son.' The look on his face was priceless."

Now that's what I call livin'!

To see photos, videos and more of the Opliger's story, please visit www.bothhands.org/opliger-family

CHAPTER 18

We Couldn't Walk that Road by Ourselves

I'm always amazed at how people come to the decision to adopt. Take Joel and Tracy Eckert, for example. Even though adoption was on their minds almost from the day they were married, they weren't in that much of a hurry. Four years into their marriage, Tracy gave birth to Anna, something of an unexpected and unplanned blessing. Once they had started their family, they thought it would be nice to have maybe two more children and then adopt. But then Joel, an attorney, began experiencing some health issues and it became clear that they would likely not be able to have any more biological children.

"Looking back, this may have been God nudging us to adopt because had we been able to have more children biologically, we might have decided our family was big enough and we wouldn't have adopted," Tracy told me. "Even after it was clear we may not be able to have more children, however, Joel was still hesitant to adopt."

Boy can I relate to Joel. While it's not always the case, husbands aren't as eager to adopt as wives, as my own reluctance will attest. But about a year after Tracy suggested they begin the adoption process in earnest, Joel came around. Two days after Christmas in 2012, he told Tracy, "Let's go ahead and start the process."

The Eckerts attended Fellowship Bible Church, where Sara and I worship. It's a church where twenty percent of the children have been adopted, so the first thing they did was meet with the children's pastor, Marty Schwieterman, who was also an adoptive parent.

Fun little side note: I've known Marty and his wife Lora since we started going there many years ago, before they had adopted. After our adoption, Marty and, Lora asked to get together with Sara and me to have coffee and learn more about the process. Marty is a huge proponent of adoption. His encouragement and enthusiasm is unmatched and he has helped many people through the adoption process. But now, he and Lora were considering adopting for themselves and Marty's hesitation was his age. "JT, I think I'm too old to be a dad again," he said. I remember looking across the table at him and just said what I was thinking, "Marty, better an old dad than no dad."

Something must have clicked because Marty and Lora started the adoption process and the next thing I knew there was the cutest little Asian girl running around our church calling him Dad. Analise has brought joy, unspeakable joy to her family and Marty continues to be the go-to guy at our church when someone is adopting.

"We were pretty clueless about the whole process and wanted to get an overview, see what our options were, whether we should adopt domestically or internationally," Tracy explained. "After meeting with our pastor and talking to our friends who had adopted, we eventually decided to adopt domestically."

During their conversation with Marty, they learned that the average cost of a domestic adoption at that time was around $20,000.

"Our initial thought was okay; we can handle that. From the very beginning, we worked hard to save money so that we could pay off Joel's law school loans quickly, and now that we had paid those off we could handle the $20,000."

They applied with an adoption agency in Utah, and learned that the cost for their adoption would be more like $30,000.

"That was a bit of a stretch for us," Tracy explained. "I sew children's clothes and started making necklaces to sell, which brought in about $1,000. It helped, but it clearly wasn't enough, and coming up with the money required wasn't going to be easy for us."

About that time, they met with a couple from church, Derek and Jennifer Bell—huge proponents of adoption. They encouraged Joel and Tracy to pursue fundraising for their adoption. Derek was the Chairman of the Board at Both Hands and recommended the Eckerts do a Both Hands project. Initially, the Eckerts resisted.

"It just didn't seem right. Joel's an attorney." Tracy thought. "We should be able to afford this. What will our friends think if we can't handle this on our own? We can do this on our own even if it means taking out a loan, something we try not to do for anything except our mortgage."

Every adoption is different, especially when it comes to the cost. So many factors go into how much money is needed to adopt, including possible medical expenses, legal costs, and the like. As things progressed for Joel and Tracy, it became clear that the total cost would reach as high as $40,000.

"We finally realized that if we were going to adopt, we would have to find a way to help us pay for it, so we turned to Both Hands and applied for their assistance," Tracy explained. "I remember thinking at the time, 'There's no way they are going to accept us. Once they see how much we earn and our personal budget they'll turn us down.'"

What Tracy didn't know was that at Both Hands, we don't want any family to go into debt in order to adopt a child. That's the whole point. The way I look at it, finances should never prevent an orphan from receiving the love and nurture of a family. We want families to bring a new child into their homes without having to worry about their finances. I also believe that a family should give their friends a chance to be a part of their child's legacy and what better way than to help raise funds needed to make it happen.

"When I got word that we were accepted by Both Hands, I was so relieved. We would have either gotten a loan or dipped into our retirement account, but this took all the pressure off us and we could focus on the adoption."

The Eckert's small group from church rallied around them as they began making plans for their Both Hands project. We helped them find Ms. Helen, a lovely widow who instantly bonded with the Eckerts—even to the point that to this day she's considered part of the family, sort of an extra Grandma.

Then everything started to happen at once.

"Our team was having a letter sending party when we got word that our agency had matched us with a birthmother in California who was due in a week-and-a-half. We were so excited as we headed off to California to get our brand new little baby, whose birthmother named her Israel."

When they got to the hospital, Joel, Tracy, and five-year-old Anna were so eager to take their baby home, only to have their case worker walk them down the hall to a little room where she gave them the news: the birthmother has changed her mind.

"We were devastated," Tracy recalled. "Joel actually collapsed, and I just cried and cried. It was so sad, compounded by the fact that we learned the birthmother was actually homeless. We still met with her and told her we loved her and would continue praying for her, but our hearts were truly broken."

They returned home without the baby they had such high hopes for and quickly realized how fortunate they were to have a team on their side.

"Somehow our Both Hands team had gotten into our house and posted encouraging Bible verses all over the place and filled our refrigerator with meals we could heat up. And then we learned that our volunteers had already raised $12,000 for us—the exact amount that we had already paid for our failed adoption in California. It reminded us how faithful the Lord is, because He knew what would happen before we traveled out there and it gave us the courage to pursue another adoption."

They joined their team a few weeks later to renovate Ms. Helen's home, and by the time all the donations came in, they had raised about $33,000.

A couple months after their project, word came in that another birthmother had been found—this time in Utah. Joel and Tracy cautiously headed off to Utah without Anna this time, praying they wouldn't experience another heartbreak. Knowing of their past experience, however, their case worker hadn't called them until the mother had relinquished her right to keep the child. They were overjoyed and speechless when they arrived in Utah and found out they had a son – and he was really theirs!

"Finally, we had our new son, and we named him Isaiah Israel Emanuel! His two middle names were given to him by his birthmother. Our team met us at the airport with balloons and flowers—it was quite a party, yet another reminder of how God had everything under control. Isaiah was the son He had for us all along."

"The cost of our adoption totaled $63,000," Tracy told me. "Without our Both Hands project, we never would have been able to adopt. I fell in love with Isaiah the first time I laid eyes on him, and still marvel at the way the Lord made it all happen. But it's really not about the money. It's about bringing a community around us because the Lord knows we aren't meant to walk the road of adoption on our own. Both Hands taught us that."

When I see Joel, Tracy, Anna and Isaiah, I'm reminded that we serve an awesome and powerful King who's not wringing His hands over the events that are happening. He loves us and I believe He loves adoption."

To see photos, videos and more of the Eckert's story, please visit www.bothhands.org/eckert-family

CHAPTER 19

A Series of Coincidences

Warning: attending a Steven Curtis Chapman concert could be hazardous to your comfort zone. Like I said before, every adoption has a turning point that it becomes very clear what God is saying.

Shortly after they were married, Luke and Katie Adams attended one of Chapman's concerts in Omaha, Nebraska. During a break in the music, a large video screen featured the story of one of Chapman's adopted children. Katie turned to her husband and declared, "We're going to do that someday."

Luke had spent a summer in China, so being the practical man that he is—he's a controller for a steel company—he agreed with his wife, suggesting that they adopt a child from China.

"In order to adopt from China, you have to be at least thirty years old," Luke told me. "We were in our early twenties at the time, so thirty seemed a long way away. But Katie kept that thought in her back pocket, so when we turned thirty, God must have spoken to her heart because she said, 'it's time.'"

"Time for what?" he asked.

"Time to start thinking about adoption again."

By this time, Katie had given birth to Finn, and Luke admits he agreed to adopt somewhat reluctantly, which as you know I can relate to. Like I said before, we guys can be a little slow to come around on adoption. But to his credit, he didn't resist like I did, and they began the process.

"Once you begin to see pictures, you realize these are real children who do not have a family," Luke explained. "That's when I went all in, eager to provide a home for one of those kids."

That always reminds me of the story of the boy walking along the beach that is littered with starfish, destined to die because they've washed ashore. He starts throwing them in the water and an older man, who has been watching him says, "Why are you working so hard at that, sonny. You can't save them all." The little boy bends down to pick up a starfish and tosses it into the water. Then he looks at the older man and simple says, "Saved that one."

Luke's eagerness would evaporate quickly. At the time, they were told the waiting period for those wanting to adopt a healthy child from China was eight years. To Katie especially, this new information was devastating. Today, you can adopt a child with special needs from China much more quickly.

"I felt I had already waited eight years from the time I first decided to adopt until Luke turned thirty. And now they were telling us we would have to wait eight more? I was pretty bummed."

They shared this unfortunate news with some friends from church who asked the obvious question: Why China? These friends suggested they consider adopting from Thailand. Here's where it gets interesting.

"One of the reasons we were so set on China is that we had friends there," Katie told me. "During the adoption process in China, adoptive parents cannot visit the child they have chosen until the adoption is complete. But we knew our friends would be able to visit the child, so it just seemed to make sense for us. We told our friends from church we would at least consider Thailand, but truthfully, our hearts weren't in it. But when we got home from church that night, we had an email from our friends in China telling us they were moving to Thailand."

Coincidence? Miracle? You decide.

The next day Luke and Katie contacted the one adoption agency they could find that would facilitate adoption for couples who were not dealing with fertility issues and learned that they had one spot available. The agency sent them a list of names and pictures, asking them to select their top five choices. The agency would then decide which of those five children would become their child.

"We weren't comfortable with that process, so we told them we had chosen one girl with special needs," Katie explained. "Yet another surprise, as the agency told us that no other couple had spoken for this child, so they would allow us to adopt her."

Within forty-eight hours of being disappointed at not being able to adopt a child from China, Luke and Katie knew who their adoptive child would be. As I've mentioned before, international adoption is fraught with bureaucracy, but it's well worth the wait. After thirty-one months of paperwork, Luke and Katie were able to travel to Thailand and claim Maya Kate as their own.

We often focus on the parents when we think about adoption, but can you imagine what it must be like for the adopted child? One day, you're in a room with seventeen beds, no bedding, and bunkmates that are always changing. The next day, you're in a bedroom with twin beds, mountains of soft, comfortable bedding, with a bunkmate who goes by the name of Mom.

That's what happened to Maya Kate, initially afraid to sleep alone, prompting Katie to temporarily sleep next to her new daughter.

"Sometimes I need a swift kick of reality to remind me that my girl came from hard places," Katie confessed. "And sometimes hard places mean a not-so-lovely day here at home. So when Maya shies away from going to bed alone, fusses because her room has 'funny sounds,' or rocks to self-soothe, I ask God to gently remind me that not too long ago my sweet girl didn't know what it meant to be home. What it meant to be part of a family."

But having a child who was afraid to sleep alone turned out to be the least of their worries. Shortly after returning from Thailand, Maya Kate began complaining of severe headaches and experiencing frightening seizures.

And sometimes hard places mean a not-so-lovely day here at home.

"We were in a panic," Katie recalled. "We contacted a specialist in another state who examined her and then told us to take her home to die—there was nothing he could do. We went to another specialist who told us essentially the same thing. Then the orthopedic surgeon I work for contacted a neurosurgeon friend of his who after examining Maya Kate, told us he would at least try to help her."

Three weeks after returning home from Thailand, little Maya Kate underwent brain surgery, which could have killed her were it not for yet another coincidence.

"Prior to her surgery, a couple of friends came over and we shaved our heads to show Maya Kate that it wouldn't hurt," Katie explained. "Then we shaved hers, and that's when we discovered a roadmap of scars on her little scalp. Clearly she had had brain surgery before, so we contacted the orphanage in Thailand to get more information. It turned out they hadn't disclosed everything to us, but after much stonewalling, they faxed her complete medical records to us, just before her scheduled surgery. Her surgeon took one look at the records and had to change his entire approach to her surgery. Had we not gotten those records in time, the surgery he had originally planned would likely have caused irreparable damage."

Today, Maya Kate is an active, joyful little girl with a good prognosis for a normal life expectancy. She has a brain injury, which sometimes affects her behavior and social skills. The doctors say she is doing much better than they ever expected, something they cannot explain.

"She loves to sing and dance," Luke proudly told me. "She's the life of the party."

Rewind a bit: what about all of those adoption expenses? That's where Judy comes in. Working with Both Hands, Luke and Katie's church found Judy, who lost her husband to cancer a few years ago. Since his death, Judy hadn't changed anything in their house—she even kept his slippers by the bed, right where he left them. So they asked her to make a list of all the things she would like to have done to her house. That list became twelve projects undertaken by forty-seven friends from church along with some local contractors. They replaced the concrete in the driveway and sidewalks. Stripped and caulked the exterior windows. Rebuilt the back deck. Replaced the basement ceiling. And much, much more.

Judy was overwhelmed. Due to her husband's failing health, their relatively nice house fell into disrepair, and she had no way to bring it back to its original condition. And as is the case with most Both Hands projects, Luke and Katie have remained in contact with her.

Luke and Katie had hoped to raise $12,000 to help pay for their adoption, and by the time they counted the last check, guess how much they had raised? If you guessed $12,000, you nailed it.

And in what has to be a "when it rains, it pours" conclusion to their story, Luke and Katie recently welcomed twins into their world, as Katie delivered Lucy and Hattie.

"We are so blessed," Katie beamed. "God has been faithful, every step of the way. I asked Finn once how our family was different before Maya came into it, and he was quick to respond: 'It used to be so quiet.' He's absolutely right. Our home has always been fun, but we laugh a lot more now. My heart still pauses in my chest sometimes when a little cocoa skinned girl calls me Mommy and asks to be held. What an absolutely amazing gift from God and to think we could have missed this."

I just don't get tired of hearing these stories. There are so many instances where God has shown up at just the right time.

My heart still pauses in my chest sometimes when a little cocoa skinned girl calls me Mommy and asks to be held.

There's one project where a family had a new shed donated, only to have the offer rescinded, but then be offered another shed from a different donor at the last minute!

We've had several projects where a widow was so moved by her project that she began to attend church regularly again.

Or the one where the family brought home their adopted son right before their project and he was able to serve the widow alongside the rest of their Both Hands team.

One of my favorite stories is the one about the volunteer on a project in Texas who realized he was serving the widow in the same community where he was arrested for operating a crack house decades earlier. At that time, the widow had walked up and down the street praying for the ones who had been arrested, him being one of them.

You can't make this stuff up!

I've learned to say, "Always amazed, never surprised."

To see photos, videos and more of the Adams' story, please visit www.bothhands.org/adams-family

CHAPTER 20

Could You Lend a Hand... or Both?

This journey began with a tragedy. One day I'm just an ordinary farm kid giving my dad a little attitude. The next day I'm an orphan. I don't believe God causes bad things to happen, but if we place our trust in Him, He will redeem those bad things and bring about something bigger and better than we could ever imagine. That's what He did for me. Knowing what it feels like to be an orphan planted a seed in my soul that would eventually lead me to help others adopt vulnerable children who have no one to care for them. Seeing my neighbors and their tractors planting our crops before they planted their own left a mark on my memory that I would use to help widows. So as much as I still miss my parents, I'm grateful that God used my loss to impact so many more lives.

But we have a lot more work to do.

Did you know that there are more than 132 million children in the world who are considered orphans?[1] Think about that for

---

1 "Orphans." UNICEF. June 2015. http://www.unicef.org/media/media_45279.html.

a minute. Almost half the population of the United States. Many of them languish in orphanages where they are often neglected for long periods of time. That's not a criticism of orphanages. Most are staffed by caring people who love children, but they operate on low budgets and do not have enough workers to give the children the attention they need.

I was lucky to have an aunt and uncle who not only took me in as their own, but gave a home to my siblings as well. Most orphans in the world aren't so fortunate. In South Asia, an orphaned child is one-third less likely to attend school than a non-orphaned child. In the Congo, that number jumps to one-half. In many countries, orphans end up on the street with no one watching over them. They become vulnerable to trafficking for cheap labor or sexual exploitation. In many African countries, they are often kidnapped by rival militias and forced to serve as child soldiers. In China, it is not unusual for abandoned children to eventually be forced into sex trafficking.[2]

I'm the one who has been blessed!

A few years ago, Bethany Christian Services, on whose Nashville board I once served, rescued a young Chinese girl who had been sent to the United States as a sex slave. That's right—child prostitution right here in the land of the free. But the good news is that a family adopted this teenager and today she's happily married and working on a master's degree.

When I see my daughter Gracie playing with her friends or doing her homework, I shudder to think where she would be today if we hadn't adopted her. More importantly, I shudder to think where I would be if we hadn't adopted her. As most people who have adopted would tell you, "I'm the one who has been blessed!" But, my heart breaks at the thought of the babies left behind; ones who right now are crying in their cribs or have

2 Hays, Jeffrey. "CHILD ABDUCTION, KIDNAPING AND TRAFFICKING IN CHINA." July 2015. http://factsanddetails.com/china/cat4/sub21/item1157.html.

stopped crying because they have learned that no one is coming to comfort them.

It's not just children overseas who need loving, caring families. In the United States, more than 100,000 children in foster care are waiting to be adopted. Sadly, 23,000 teens "age out" every year. They become legal adults at age eighteen and enter the real world completely on their own. Without the support of a family, they often struggle. Approximately twenty-five percent become homeless within eighteen months of leaving foster care. By the time they are twenty-four years old, half will be unemployed. Less than three percent will earn a college degree, and seventy-one percent of the women will be pregnant by the time they're twenty-one.[3] Wouldn't it be great if in your county not a single foster child aged out because of a surplus of families willing to adopt these children? There are some places in America where that is happening, thanks to groups who have answered the call to care for the least of these.

All these orphans need is a chance, and their best chance comes from a family that will adopt them.

All these orphans need is a chance, and their best chance comes from a family that will adopt them. Maybe *your* family.

Then there's another category of children who would benefit from the love of an adopting family: infants who are the result of an unplanned pregnancy. Tragically, approximately one million pregnancies annually are terminated through abortion.[4] The good news is that pro-life agencies have seen increasing success in counseling women to carry their babies to full term so that they may be adopted. In order to continue that trend, however, they

3 Soronen, Rita. "We Are Abandoning Children in Foster Care." CNN. April 17, 2014. http://www.cnn.com/2014/04/16/opinion/soronen-foster-children/.

4 "Induced Abortion in the United States." Guttmacher Institute. September 2016. https://www.guttmacher.org/fact-sheet/induced-abortion-united-states.

need families who will step up to the plate and open their homes to these babies.

So open your left hand right now and take a look at it. Could you imagine holding a child in that hand—one that you have adopted into your family? Remember, adoption was "invented" by God, as all of us have been adopted into His family through the sacrificial love and obedience of Jesus. If you're like I was and are listing off all the reasons why you are unable to adopt, you can cross this reason off right now: "We can't afford to adopt." Because I know someone who can help.

A widow.

There are approximately 13.6 million widows in the United States. Every year, 700,000 women lose their spouses and will remain widows for an average of fourteen years.[5] Seventy-five percent of widows lose their support base after the death of their husbands, meaning they have no one close by to turn to for simple things like help getting groceries, upkeep and maintenance of their homes, and health care.[6] The trauma of losing a lifelong partner often results in depression and isolation. Simple tasks seem too daunting to perform. No one's around to fix a leaky faucet, repair a crumbling porch, or carry the trash to the curb. In one of our Both Hands projects, a widow could not bring herself to enter her garage after her husband passed away. There's a good chance that within a mile of where you live, a lonely, discouraged widow is wondering how she's going to pay for a new roof or just replace a light bulb in her laundry room.

So now I'd like you to open your right hand and take a close look at it. Could you imagine a few blisters from scraping and painting a widow's house? Would you be willing to get that hand dirty pulling weeds and planting shrubs to turn a widow's yard into

---

5 "These Are The Statistics." Widows Hope. http://www.widowshope.org/first-steps/these-are-the-statistics/.

6 Elwert, Felix, and Nicholas A. Christakis. "Variation in the Effect of Widowhood on Mortality by the Causes of Death of Both Spouses." American Journal of Public Health. November 2008. http://www.ncbi.nlm.nih.gov/pmc/articles/PMC2636447/.

something she enjoys looking at? Imagine the comfort and pure joy your grandmother, your mom or anyone you know who has lost a spouse would experience in being shown they have not been forgotten.

Since God nudged me off the cliff eight years ago, Both Hands has brought 735 orphans into forever families and served 665 widows. In my wildest dreams—and I'm a half-full kind of guy—I wouldn't have thought we could have accomplished so much in such a short time. What began as an experiment in my hometown has grown into a ministry with over 600 projects completed across forty-two states. And we're just getting started because our numbers grow every weekend! You can check out BothHandsBook.com to see where we are today.

Along the way, we've had the chance to collaborate with many great organizations who all have a heart for doing something about the orphan crisis. Lifesong for Orphans has been our closest friend and partner. They have referred many families to us. In fact, during those early years, it's safe to say that Lifesong was our lifeline to the adoption community and they played a key role in keeping Both Hands going.

There's another organization called the Christian Alliance for Orphans (CAFO), which is an umbrella organization that most faith-based orphan-related groups are members. If you want to know more about those groups, check out our additional pages with next steps in the back of this book.

Jedd Medefind, President of CAFO, has found some shocking numbers in his book *Becoming Home*. First, only two out of every five practicing Christians has even considered adoption and almost twenty-five percent have either no desire to adopt or think it's too expensive. Too expensive? I think we've got that excuse covered.

There's a lot of good work to be done. If you want to join us, we have plenty of opportunities for you to serve. A Both Hands project is truly a win-win-win-win experience. First, a widow's life is dramatically improved through the generosity of a volunteer work team. Second, an orphan receives the wonderful gift of a family. Third, the adoptive family experiences the joy of welcoming a new son or daughter - or both! Fourth, all the people who receive a letter in the mail, asking them to sponsor a volunteer have an opportunity to do something that God calls all us to do; take care of widows and orphans. And as a bonus, everyone who volunteers to work comes away feeling great, despite the blisters and sore muscles. I can honestly say that every Both Hands project I've ever been a part of is nothing but FUN! Just a bunch of people walking around smiling and working.

Now look down at both of your open hands. One for the widow. One for the orphan. We could use those hands to help us reduce the number of orphans and improve the lives of widows. When you do something to help both, you are practicing religion that is "pure and faultless." (James 1:27 NIV). At Both Hands, we have a lot of fun in the process.

One other interesting aspect of Both Hands is how we set it up. I thought it was a no-brainer to have one hundred percent of all the funds that were received for a family's project, go towards adoption expenses. That's right…and not take anything out for the operations of Both Hands. Most people thought we were crazy, but something told me to try to make that happen. That would mean we would essentially be operating like missionaries, having to raise our own support. Admittedly, the first few years were pretty lean, but we've still been able to keep that pledge. Like I said, I have learned to trust that God will provide for our needs, and He has.

Two years after I started Both Hands, I received a letter from Corbin McGuire, a good friend who I once tried to bring on to our recruiting business. With his permission, I'm closing this book with an excerpt from it because it captures my vision for Both Hands along with the risk that comes whenever we obey God:

JT,

Isn't it amazing that you could die today and all the people would talk about at your funeral is what you have done for the last two years. In other words, nothing you have done up until the last two years is even in the same ballpark. It's amazing that it only takes a few different choices to make such a large, profound, eternal impact.

I want you and Sara to understand something. Because of the difference you are making, if I were Satan I would target you and try to take you out.

- *I would see if I could disqualify you. I would get you into sin so no one would believe your message. Now you would be in National Enquirer. Making all these great claims but you have no integrity whatsoever.*

- *If I couldn't disqualify you, I would distract you. I would get your focus back on material things and making money so that you couldn't be concerned about making an eternal impact.*

- *If I couldn't distract you, I would divide you. I would try to create arguments, disagreements, anger among your organization to make you a joke.*

- *If I couldn't divide you, I would discourage you. I would get you so down under heartache that you would give up.*

- *If I couldn't do that, I would endanger you. I would make you love your life. I would get you scared.*

- *If I lost all those, I would try to kill you.*

So you become the bull's eye. You become the authentication. Armor up JT. You aren't playing a mundane game of recruiting or book sales. You are messing with Satan's souls. It's a whole new level. You aren't alone though. Romney and I are in the boat praying with you.

167

I'm not totally sure why this letter fires me up, but it does. Maybe it's because I've got this picture in my mind of Satan and his minions starting each day, making their plans. When they get to my name, I don't want them checking off the box that says "not a threat." I want them saying "Oh nuts! He's up again!" Folks, this is Hotel Earth. We're not here forever and we've got to make a difference in any way we can while we're here. Things rot! Life-changing impact lasts!

Have there been some difficult things since we started down this path? Yes and I imagine there will be more. But the farther out on the limb I get, the safer I feel. I have flat out learned to trust God.

Listen, I'm not sure where you are in life, but my prayer is this resonates with you. Perhaps you're in a tragic or challenging situation. I hope as you read this, you see that as tough as it may be, God may be equipping you for something big and to take that leap of faith. Might be some heat ahead, but where there is heat, there is refinement.

If you've experienced death in such a close way as I have, you also know how valuable your loved ones are and those who have surrounded you during those incredibly hard times. Know that although it may not be evident or explainable in that moment, our God is all knowing, all-powerful, and is aware of exactly what we need.

Maybe you or someone you know is in the midst of an unplanned pregnancy. I hope you realize that there are some very positive options and most likely some huge blessings in store for you. God tells us that all life has value - yours and that child's included.

If you're a man in this situation, I hope you see that you need to take responsibility for your actions. I see this as one of the biggest challenges facing our country today.

In any case, you need to realize that even though you're not always in control of your circumstances, you are the one in control of your attitude. Nobody else is. Maybe you need an Uncle Ralph to grab you by the arm and say, "Stop feeling sorry for yourself."

If that's you, I have a challenge for you...say out loud, ten times: "I'm alert, alive, friendly, cordial, firm, and enthusiastic!" Put down this book. I'm serious. Ok, maybe read the phrase over a couple more times and then put the book down. There is no way you can do that little exercise and not feel just a little bit better. Now say it like you mean it!

Maybe you're unhappy in your career. Could be a couple of things happening. Maybe God is using that opportunity to help you develop some skills or contacts that will be useful later in life. In that case, best to quit the whining and embrace the challenges. Start counting your blessings and not your problems.

Or it could be that you need to leave that business and do something that's more in your area of gifting. I've found that when someone does something in their gifting, it's not work. Maybe there are opportunities looking you in the eye and you just need to go for it, make a plan, and execute. Just get out of the driveway, man!

Maybe you are thinking about adopting. Maybe it's your only option, but if it's not you should also know it doesn't have to be Plan B. It should also be clear by now that the financial part shouldn't be an obstacle either. Why let any amount of money stand between you and God's calling? From watching so many adoptions and Both Hands projects, I've observed that God provides the funds, one way or another.

Whatever your excuse is for hesitating, whether it's being too old like Marty, or worried about the finances like me, or any others you can think of, God's in control. Like I mentioned, we're not all called to adopt, but James 1:27 tells us that we're all called to care for widows and orphans.

If you'd like to climb into the boat with us, like Corbin mentioned—whether you're planning to adopt or just want to help others who do—check us out at BothHandsBook.com.

I think we could probably find a pen, a letter and a pair of gloves for you.

NEXT STEPS

Visit www.BothHandsBook.com today!

ADOPTION:

If you are considering adoption but don't know what questions to ask, please visit www.bothhandsbook.com for information on funding sources, adoption agencies, and much more.

GET INVOLVED WITH BOTH HANDS:

There are many ways people can jump on board:

- Apply to do a Both Hands project for your adoption.

- Volunteer on a project in your area. If you're not adopting but still want to do a project, you can raise funds for another orphan cause, an adoption fund, or to help Both Hands continue the vision.

- Donate to Both Hands to help serve more orphans and widows or even become a monthly supporter at www.bothhands.org/give or by mail to Both Hands, P.O. Box 2713, Brentwood, TN 37024.

SPEAKING:

JT is a phenomenal speaker with over thirty years in team-building and storytelling. He's given talks at conferences, churches, fundraisers, and other events across the country. His topics include his journey from pain to passion through Both Hands, advocating the sanctity of life, growing a healthy marriage, encouraging entrepreneurs to pursue their calling, coaching leaders on building a strong organizational culture and more.

Learn more at www.bothhands.org/speaking.

BOOK STUDY:

Finally, you can download discussion questions for a book study with your small group and purchase additional books and discount packages.

RESOURCES:

Here's additional information for organizations who have impacted Both Hands:

- Bethany Christian Services: www.bethany.org

- Show Hope: www.showhope.org

- Lifesong for Orphans: www.lifesongfororphans.org

- Christian Alliance for Orphans (CAFO): www.cafo.org

- Southwestern Company: www.southwestern.com

- The Halftime Institute: www.halftimeinstitute.org

- Meals on Wheels: www.mowaa.org
- Modern Widows Club: www.modernwidowsclub.com
- Sweet Sleep: www.sweetsleep.org
- Abba Fund: www.abbafund.org

ACKNOWLEDGMENTS

I have been blessed to have many great men and women pour into my life and help me become who I am. I only hope I have paid it forward faithfully.

One of the things I appreciated most about Southwestern was their commitment to teaching young people positive principals to live by and ethical selling methods. One of those philosophies I bought hook, line, and sinker was best expressed by Edwin Markham. He said, "There is a destiny that makes us brothers. No one goes his way alone; All that we send into the lives of others, Comes back into our own."

When I think of acknowledging people, the first thought that comes to my mind is to thank God for giving me breath and the talents I possess. Job 33:4 says, "The Spirit of God has made me; the breath of the Almighty gives me life." It's pretty simple for me.

Not to pile on, but in Psalms 139:13, it says, " For you formed my inward parts; you knitted me together in my mother's womb." You gotta give credit where it's due.

The next person is who I would refer to as the unsung hero of Both Hands; my wife. I've been married to Sara Olson for 32 years and yes, I outkicked my coverage, married up, however you want to say it. I am truly a lucky man. She's been my chief encourager, through all the ups and downs of raising five children. Through the trials and tribulations of starting a business and then a non-profit. She stood by me through my stupid mistakes and still has provided my chief need: to be respected.

When we started Both Hands, she left her hearts desire, to homeschool our kids, and took a job to help support our family. In those eight years, she has worked her way to a Senior VP role at Concerned Women for America. She gets very little recognition for her role in making our dream a possibility. I hope this tribute sheds some light on her importance in serving widows and orphans.

I want to thank my children, Jeff Jr., Daley, Nick, Max, and of course, Gracie for letting me share the most important parts of their lives. It's an honor to be your dad and I'm proud of each and every one of you.

I also need to thank my Aunt Marie Ann and Uncle Ralph along with all my brothers and sisters, John, Jim, Sue, Lori, Julie, Jerene, and Sandy, for tremendous support in this adventure. The style and theme of this book did not lend itself to the character development they deserve, but the role they have played in my life is epic.

Lifesong for Orphans has had and continues to play a huge role in our success. Thank you Gary and Marla Ringger, Andy Lehman, Kory Kaeb, Rich Metcalfe and the whole team for supporting us through those early years and sharing the dream of no child without a family.

There were many people at Southwestern who not only helped me develop over the years but have played an important role in funding this crazy idea. My boss for 18 years, Fred Prevost, has always been there as a great friend and confidante. His wife, Pam Prevost has been an integral part of our growth. Allen Clements, for leading me to Christ, as well as Spencer Hayes, Jerry Heffel, Dan Moore, Jeff Hawley, Rich Smith, Tom MacAuliffe, Roy Loftin, Dave Causer, and the late Creig Soeder.

I'm thankful to Bethany Christian Services for letting me be in charge of the fundraiser that produced that infamous letter from Bill Iverson. Thank you Bill, for your heart and the courage to speak what's on your mind.

Without Sweet Sleep, the non-profit started by Jen Gash, there would have been no mission trip for Don Meyer and consequently no reason to figure out a way to raise $70,000. Thank you Don Meyer and Mary Meyer for having the courage to adopt 4 kids, and to give the Both Hands concept a 'go.' Your early support of Both Hands was critical and sacrificial.

Thank you Julie Gumm for giving Both Hands a whole chapter in your book *How to Adopt Without Debt* and for the shout-out on the Dave Ramsey Show.

Thank you Jedd Medefind and the folks at Christian Alliance for Orphans for blowing wind in our sails and bringing the orphan crisis to the forefront.

Thank you Bob Buford, Dick Gygi and Greg Murtha for all your work at Halftime and for helping me get a handle on how to get Both Hands started.

For the last 19 years, I've attended Fellowship Bible Church where the Word of God is preached. I've been challenged by Jeff Schulte, Lloyd Shadrach, Bill Wellons, and Michael Easley to figure out a way to give my life away. Tom Clagett, Marty Schwieterman and Brian Petak have added their support with the use of facilities and walking with me from the beginning. They've all helped promote Both Hands publicly and privately. What a gift this congregation has been!

Corbin McGuire wrote a letter to me that is still taped to the wall by my desk. That letter has served to remind me that I must decrease and God must increase. It reminds me that this life is temporary, not our final destination and that we've got work to do, a battle to fight, and a King that's worthy of our praise. Thank you, Corbin. You inspire me to be a better man.

So grateful for Steven Curtis and Mary Beth Chapman, not just for their introduction and endorsement, but for the prayers they offered along with Dan and Terri Coley concerning our adoption journey. Those two families, along with so many others in our community have set an example that's impacted literally thousands. A bunch of kids have families because of Show Hope and all the work the Chapmans have done.

We have been blessed with an outstanding Board of Directors. Thank you all past and present Board members for your time and expertise in guiding us for the last eight years. That would include Kevin Foley, operations genius, both Don Meyer and

Mary Meyer, Marty Roe, Martha Carpenter, Teri Froman, and Joel Eckert. Thank you Derek Bell for your leadership as our chairman. Thank you Jennifer Bell, Derek's wife, for single-handedly being responsible for about 20 projects in Tennessee. She's our biggest advocate!

Special thanks go to Board member Greg Murtha. For the last five years he's been battling Stage 4 colon cancer, but that has never slowed down his enthusiasm for what we do or his ability to encourage me. His journey has led him to start a non-profit called Leading with a Limp. If you want to be inspired, check it out.

There is one more Board member that would deserve some special recognition. That would be Ty Osman and his business partner, Gregg Turner. Two of the most generous men I know who run a commercial construction company called Solomon Builders. Since the inception of Both Hands, they have given us office space, and I would emphasize the word 'given.' Great to be surrounded by people who believe in you and are willing to put some skin in the game.

I would be remiss if I didn't point out the role that my neighbors and Board members, Marty and his wife Robin, along with Ty Osman and his wife, Nancy have played in making Both Hands a success. Since we started Both Hands and Sara went to work, there have been hundreds of times that these families have played the role of parents to Gracie. Truth is she's got three sets of parents and we're very grateful for the team effort shown by all the Dream Street families.

I would also like to thank Lyn Cryderman for his guidance in helping me put all my thoughts together so it might make some sense. Thanks to Bruce Barbour for playing a key role in publishing and getting us to the finish line. And if you're reading this book because you heard about it in the media, you can thank Morgan Canclini and Two PR.

Last, but probably most important is the staff at Both Hands. It's incredible what God has allowed us to accomplish with such a small staff. I'm surrounded by three millennials who keep me current and have spent many hours on helping us put this project together.

Aimee Sipe is the Director of Operations and keeps us all moving in the right direction and on the same page. When she came on board with Both Hands she said she and Ryan did not plan to have kids… until she met all of the Both Hands families and fell in love with the idea. It's been a joy to watch her grow into this position and at the same time get married to Ryan and give birth to beautiful Sierra. Our growth over the last five years is a direct result of her leadership and guidance.

Jared DeLong is our marketing genius whose work you've enjoyed if you've seen our videos or have been moved by any of our stories and other content. He reminds us all of why we do this and has probably spent the most time on this project. Thank you, Jared!

Bethany Purdy is my assistant and Family Project Manager. She is the person all the families rely on to keep their projects on track. By the time their project is over, they all love her.

Lots of volunteers have helped us with the details of running a non-profit, but no other volunteer can match Carol Worsham. She has bought her accounting expertise to Both Hands for the last 6 years and we are so thankful for her heart for widows and orphans.

In addition to some of the people mentioned above, there are hundreds of others who have helped keep the lights on at Both Hands. I wish I could list all of them, but here are several who have been pillars in keeping the vision alive. Thank you Jeff and Amy Dobyns, Todd Prevost, Brock and Naomi Ketcher, Van and Lisa Fletcher, Danny and Frances McPherson, Chris Kirkland, Chad Jackson and the Jackson Family Foundation, Greg Buzek and Retail Orphan Initiative, Rick and Melissa Carlson, Shayna Gunn and the Churchill Foundation, Mark and Devin Floyd, Bill Strong, Paul and Terry Sanderson, Tim Swett, Hunter and

Kristin Murray, Brendan and Tisha Thiessen, Charlie and Angela Lathrop, Chris and Michelle Rew, Phil and Becky Naish, JT and Annie Thomas, John and Darien Schlegel, Dick and Jennifer Justmann, Kevin Lenci, Todd and Maria Meister, Russell and Jenny Crouch, Tom and Beth Moore, John Sommers, Phil and Joanie McLeod, Bob and Julie Weil, Jeff and Mary Lee Hansmann, Tim and Julie O'Neil, Francisco and Kasia Armada, Jerene and Rick Briggs, Jimmy and Allison Thomas and Jim and Harriet McKee.

Finally, thank you to all the families that possessed the courage to do Both Hands project. I know it takes a lot of work, but I hope you've been blessed. Thank you to the widows who have been willing to let all those families work on your house. And thank you to all the people who have donated to those projects. You've made a difference that will have generational impact.

Well done good and faithful Servants!

After being orphaned as a child alongside his four siblings, JT Olson's personal tragedy gave him an overwhelming understanding of the need to find loving homes for the world's orphaned and vulnerable children.

While drifting from party to party in college, God began to transform Olson's life. Peers introduced him to the Southwestern Company, where he spent 23 years in sales management and teambuilding and eventually met his wife, Sara. After Southwestern, JT went on to start a successful recruiting firm in Nashville, TN. Ten years later, in 2008, he followed God's calling to start Both Hands, a faith-based nonprofit serving orphans, widows and adoptive families.

With over 153 million orphans worldwide and the costs of adoption on the rise, Both Hands' goal is to fulfill the James 1:27 call to care for orphans and widows by alleviating the financial burden facing families considering adoption.

"Religion that God our Father accepts as pure and faultless is this: to look after orphans and widows in their distress and to keep oneself from being polluted by the world." (James 1:27 NIV)

Both Hands helps families raise funds for their adoptions by serving widows in their communities. In its first eight years, the organization has completed over 600 projects across 42 states that have raised over $7 million in donations for adoptions and orphan causes. More than 700 widows have received free improvements to their homes, and almost 800 orphans have been brought into forever families because of Both Hands' efforts. And the best part is, these numbers grow every weekend.

JT is a sensational speaker and an avid proponent of adoption, the pro-life movement and orphan care. He has given talks on a wide range of topics, including God's transformation of pain into passion through his journey to Both Hands, advocating the sanctity of life, to advice for couples on growing a healthy marriage, encouraging dreamers and entrepreneurs to pursue their calling, and coaching leaders on building a strong organizational culture. For information on booking JT for speaking engagements, please visit www.bothhands.org/speaking

JT and Sara have been married for over 30 years and have five children (four bio and one chosen): Jeff, Daley, Nick, Max & Grace. They now reside in Brentwood, TN, just south of Nashville. For more information about Both Hands visit www. bothhands.org, and follow JT's outreach on socials: fb.com/BothHandsFoundation and @GiveBothHands on Instagram and Twitter.